TOTAL COMPETITIVENESS

TOTAL COMPETITIVENESS

The 7 key questions for re-engineering — where you are, where you want to be and how to get there

Maurice Hardaker

McGRAW-HILL BOOK COMPANY

London · New York · St Louis · San Francisco · Auckland
Bogotá · Caracas · Lisbon · Madrid · Mexico
Milan · Montreal · New Delhi · Panama · Paris · San Juan
São Paulo · Singapore · Sydney · Tokyo · Toronto

Published by
McGRAW-HILL Book Company Europe
Shoppenhangers Road, Maidenhead, Berkshire SL6 2QL, England
Telephone 01628 23432
Fax 01628 770224

British Library Cataloguing in Publication Data
Hardaker, Maurice
   Total Competitiveness: 7 Key Questions
   for Re-engineering – Where You are,
   Where You Want to be and How to Get There
   I. Title
   658.4012

   ISBN 0-07-707992-2

Library of Congress Cataloging-in-Publication Data
Hardaker, Maurice,
   Total competitiveness: the 7 key questions for re-engineering–
   where you are, where you want to be, and how to get there / Maurice
   Hardaker.
      p.   cm.
   Includes index.
   ISBN 0-07-707992-2
   1. Competition.   2. Industrial management.   3. Success in
   business.   I. Title.
   HD41.H298
   658.4'063–dc20   94–39565
                                                                              CIP

234 BL 9765

Typeset by BookEns Ltd, Royston, Herts.
and printed and bound in Great Britain by Biddles Ltd., Guildford, Surrey.

Printed on permanent paper in compliance with ISO Standard 9706

Contents

Contents

Preface

This book is to help senior managers find out how to make their enterprises better — more competitive, more effective, even radically different. *They* find out; the senior managers. Nobody else can tell them. There are no trendy off-the-shelf solutions. No two-minute fixes. This is basic, pragmatic top management Do It Yourself.

The approach is practical and down-to-earth. It is based on answering just seven deceptively simple and logically connected questions. Only the top management team can answer them. It is always a struggle, but well worth the two to three days of effort needed to do it. The answers reveal the unique opportunities to that specific enterprise at that particular time. And the opportunities *are* unique.

One day, Albert Einstein arrived late to hand out some examination papers in mathematics. He rushed into his office, grabbed the papers and rushed out, hotly pursued by his secretary, shouting, 'Herr Professor! Herr Professor! You have the wrong papers! Those are the questions you asked them last year!' Einstein shouted back, 'It doesn't matter. I've changed the answers!''

The answers to the seven questions here may be different next year, or in ten years, but the questions will remain the same.

The techniques described in this book are all derived from my work with senior- and top-management teams in hundreds of enterprises over the past 25 years, commercial and non-commercial. This is also the source of many of the examples quoted, augmented by stories from business publications such as the *Financial Times*, the *Harvard Business Review*, *The*

ix

Economist, The Wall Street Journal, Business Week, and many others. These many examples from the real world, whether from my own work or from the reports of others, are drawn from a wide variety of industries in Europe, the United States, and Japan (there must be wonderful, innovative things happening in Australasia and South America, too, for example, but, sadly, I have not yet experienced them).

The examples serve two purposes. The first is to illustrate a point being discussed. The second, and more important, is to serve as a mental stimulant to the reader, not necessarily to copy exactly, but perhaps to exclaim, 'Hmmm. Maybe we could ... ?' Computers don't get good ideas, only people do. The origin of competitiveness is that marvellous, mysterious, complicated, and potentially creative organ between your ears. The book's purpose is to provide a structured approach for collective, creative top-management thinking.

The approach is not only cross-industry, it applies to any size of enterprise — large or small, a complete business or government department or a unit of one, a national or a global corporation.

Einstein once said, 'Things should always be made as simple as possible. But not any simpler.' The seven questions at the centre of this approach are as simple as I can make them, but they are far from trivial. The result is an approach that I believe to be timeless, not tied to any particular passing management fad or fashion. This is as it should be because competitiveness is going to be with us for a long time.

Part 1

INTRODUCTION

1
Total Competitiveness and business re-engineering

'Business re-engineering' is a term that has entered the business lexicon only recently. Michael Hammer popularized it in his seminal *Harvard Business Review* article, 'Re-engineering Work: Don't Automate, Obliterate' (July–August 1990). Since then, it has been embraced like other terms have been, such as 'Total Quality Management' or being 'market-driven' or 'customer-driven', and so forth. Like them, it can lead to a lot of top management sloganeering, and not much action.

But it *can* have a massive impact on business success.

Business re-engineering needs top management leadership and ownership (as should Total Quality Management, and the rest of those good things) because it should challenge the status quo of the entire enterprise. It usually requires large amounts of money, information technology, and patience. It normally demands seismic organizational changes. So it needs that lead and drive by a committed top-management team, to bring it off.

A Total Competitiveness study using the techniques described in this book will almost certainly result in a need for 're-engineering'. But it will be a consequence of finding the unique competitive opportunities, rather than the reason to look for them. 'Let's re-engineer our business!' is not a good way to start. Instead, 'Let's find ways in which to become

3

more competitive!' is the approach advocated in this book. Then, the requirement for any re-engineering will be associated with an identified, compelling business need. And it will have been identified by the top-management team.

The means of becoming more competitive need not have any particular label, such as 're-engineering'. Many examples will be described that resulted in an increase in competitiveness, but which are not re-engineering. Such opportunities should be exploited like any other.

Many examples of companies that *have* re-engineered their business, to a greater or lesser extent, will also be described here. A lot of them effectively re-engineered before the term was invented. They make fine exemplars for business re-engineering, after the event, but they did what they did to become more competitive. Equally, they were not aware of the techniques described in this book. Like the techniques of re-engineering themselves, those described here grew out of my observations of what worked in a wide variety of industries and different enterprises. The results of these observations have been distilled into a structured approach that is applicable to any enterprise — commercial or non-commercial — wanting to get better at doing what it *should* be doing, to put it in the simplest terms.

Nevertheless, in the environment of the middle 1990s, the term re-engineering has a precise meaning from which we can benefit. At the very least, a clear definition will enable us to distinguish between what is worthwhile and re-engineering, from what may *also* be worthwhile, but definitely is *not* re-engineering.

Two definitions

We'll start with two definitions.

First, a definition of re-engineering. This is from *Re-engineering The Corporation* by Michael Hammer (who also first used the term) and James Champy (Harper Business, 1993).

> '**Re-engineering is the fundamental re-thinking** and **radical re-design** of business processes to achieve dramatic improvements in critical contemporary measures of performance, such as cost, quality, service, and speed.'

Now a definition of Total Competitiveness.

> '**Total Competitiveness is the result of multiplying:**
>
> 1 **relative product price performance and**
> 2 **relative customer satisfaction with all "customer-visible" business processes.'**
>
> '**Relative' here means relative to the competition.**

Each of the two factors in this definition is on a scale of 0 to 1.

The definition of Total Competitiveness is the lynch pin around which all the logic and techniques given in this book turn. Notice that Total Competitiveness is what the *customer* says it is.

Notice also that the definition of business re-engineering is not industry-specific. However, the concept of Total Competitiveness applies mainly to commercial enterprises, where the customer has the choice of whether or not to buy. A small change, to be described shortly, makes the concept appropriate to non-commercial enterprises, such as the Civil Service, Government departments, the police, and so forth.

From its definition, it is clear that business re-engineering is about exploiting opportunities to make dramatic improvements in the business *processes* of the enterprise. Total Competitiveness shows how the two major categories of business process — those that customers see or directly experience (the 'customer-visible' processes) and all of the others (the 'invisible' processes) — combine to give a measure of the Total Competitiveness of the enterprise.

The trick is to find which process (or combination of

processes, customer-visible and/or invisible) offers the biggest opportunities for business re-engineering or other opportunities to improve Total Competitiveness. The definition of Total Competitiveness contains the means of *measuring* it (you only have to ask your customers the right questions about relative product/service price performance and how well you compare in the customer-visible business processes — *all* of them). If your Total Competitiveness is low, you can see *why* it is low relative to your competitors. The techniques described in this book will then reveal the latent re-engineering and other opportunities open to you.

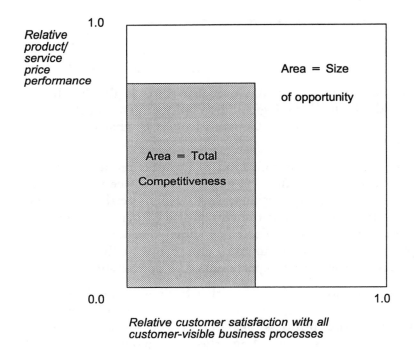

Figure 1.1 The opportunity for competitiveness

Figure 1.1 shows one way in which you can display the size of the opportunity.

The value of the first factor — relative product/service price performance — is entered on the vertical axis. In Figure 1.1, it is about 0.75. The value of the second factor — relative customer satisfaction with all customer-visible processes — is plotted on the horizontal axis. In this case, it is about 0.45. Multiply the two and we have a measure of Total Competitiveness, represented by the area of the shaded rectangle. The amount of white space remaining within the square is a measure of the size of the opportunity to improve. Try it for your own enterprise. Make even a rough guess at the sizes of the two factors that determine Total Competitiveness (then you might try positioning your major competitors on the same square to see how your area compares with theirs).

Note that the word 'enterprise' will be used throughout this book so that it may be applied to the commercial and non-commercial sectors; to an entire corporation, a country organization, a business unit, a hospital, a laboratory, an education centre, whatever. Similarly, the word 'product' will be used to mean 'product and/or service'.

Customers and consumers

In some industries, it is necessary to distinquish between customer-visible and *consumer*-visible business processes. For example, it is not usual for the ultimate user to buy detergents from Proctor and Gamble, or a Mars Bar from Mars Confectionery. These two manufacturers, and their competitors, sell their products to wholesalers or directly to large retail outlets, supermarkets, and so forth. *They* are their customers, the people who pay Proctor and Gamble and Mars Confectionery for their products. And Proctor and Gamble and Mars have to have excellent customer-visible processes to support these business relationships. But Proctor and Gamble and Mars do not stop there. They spend huge amounts of money on advertising and promoting their products. These processes of advertising and promotion are aimed directly at consumers, to whom they are highly visible, to persuade them to select their products when they shop. To measure Total Competitiveness, the relative quality of their *consumer*-visible processes has to be included with their *customer*-visible processes, which will largely be invisible to the consumer who actually uses the detergents or eats the Mars Bar.

In contrast, someone in the business of manufacturing paper-clips, for example, may choose to consider *only* the customer-visible processes. The end–user possibly has no idea who makes them, and is probably not even interested.

If you work in an industry where consumer-visible processes are important, you will know it. And you will know who are your *customers*, the people who directly pay you money in exchange for your goods or services. Perhaps the two types of visible business processes could be combined and called 'market-visible' processes. It does not matter, in principle, so long as the distinction is made between what is visible in the community to which you are selling — where there is choice and where direct comparisons can be made with competitors — and what is not visible, and where such comparisons cannot be directly made by outsiders.

Product price performance

Of course, it is necessary to discriminate between different customer segments when considering product price perfor-mance. For someone selling luxury saloon cars, 'relative to competition' means Mercedes, Jaguar, Lexus, BMW and so on. The Mercedes sales representative is not usually involved in price performance comparisons with the Fiat Uno. The latter has a different set of competitors to worry about.

It is also necessary to define what it is about the *product* that is different to the *customer-visible processes*.

If it appears on the invoice, it is product. The distinction is that simple. For example, customer education and training are part of the product if the customer has to pay for them. Customers should include them in their *price* performance comparisons. If it is not on the invoice, then 'educate and train customers' is a customer-visible business process, and its quality will be compared with that of other competing sellers who also do not charge for it. It therefore becomes part of the seller's relative *cost* performance. The customer pays for product; the seller pays for customer-visible processes.

It is important that *both* of the Total Competitiveness factors are measured from the perspective of the *customer*. But many customers simply concentrate on product price performance — it is easier. It is the seller's responsibility to ensure that the customer includes customer-visible process quality in their comparisons with competing sellers, and that the customer acknowledges the superior performance of yours. Of course, you have to *make* them excellent. And that may be an important part of any business process re-engineering projects.

The product, as we have seen, is what the customer actually pays for. While product price performance is always a key factor when buyers decide between sellers, the quality of customer-visible processes is an equally important factor. You should constantly be searching for innovative ways to enlarge and improve the service content of your customer-visible processes.

It is important to stick to the scale 0 to 1 when measuring the two factors that contribute to Total Competitiveness, as the following example shows. Suppose a particular seller is acknowledged by its customers to have the best product price performance in its industry. If just *one* customer-visible process is bad enough, Total Competitiveness can effectively be zero, despite the (acknowledged) superb product price performance. One multiplied by zero is zero. This is a harsh definition, but it is a realistic one.

How to lose customers

A large survey (on the service industry) carried out in the United States by the Forum Corporation in 1991, looked at the reasons customers leave. It also revealed why they stay.

Introduction

Six ways to lose customers:

- **1 per cent die**
- **3 per cent move away**
- **5 per cent form other friendships**
- **9 per cent for competitive reasons**
- **14 per cent because of dissatisfaction with the product**
- **68 per cent because of attitude of indifference to the customer by some employee.**

So, over two-thirds go because some customer-visible aspect of the business is being performed badly. And it is not always the apparent indifference of some employees. You may spend a fortune on developing and making superb, low-cost, new products. But all of that money can be wasted if just one customer-visible process is bad enough, such as 'deliver products'.

If a customer in Helsinki gets the wrong product, late, incomplete and damaged, at the wrong address and with Arabic documentation, the customer might well be tempted to consider a different supplier, even if it involves a compromise on product price performance.

Notice that the people influencing the change of supplier might be different to the people who made the product price performance comparison. Very senior people may have made the best strategic choice between sellers, but if there is an awful 'deliver products' process, it is the customer's people in the Goods Receiving department who suffer. Similarly, a poor quality 'bill customers' process creates pain (and additional cost) in the customer's Accounts Payable department. If the people there have to spend hours and days each month reconciling confusing and inaccurate invoices, the noise level and bitterness will eventually reach the executive floor.

Again, operations people will be influencing a strategic decision, *possibly to the detriment of the buyer, as well as to the*

10

seller. It can change from a win-win situation, where the buyer and seller both win (much the best), to a lose-lose one (much the worst).

Customer-visible processes, therefore, are important. The fact that many companies largely ignore them — as buyer as well as seller — provides a splendid opportunity for finding ways of increasing Total Competitiveness.

Customer-visible process excellence

Product price performance *must* be 'relative to competitors' in your segment. This, after all, is the basis of the customer's price performance decision. The only opinion of value in this 'benchmarking' is the customer's. Now, consider the second factor, the quality of customer-visible processes. Here are some examples of customer-visible processes:

- 'bill customers'
- 'maintain/service installed products'
- 'deliver products'
- 'offer products for sale'
- 'advertise products'
- 'announce new products'.

The *customer* should compare the performance of your customer-visible processes with those of your competitors. This is how you can get a measure of the second factor contributing to your Total Competitiveness. *But you should compare yourself with the 'best of breed'*. This is a much more valuable benchmark as it reveals the potential for improvement. Find out who is best in the world at the process 'deliver products', for example. It may be someone totally outside of your industry. If this is the case, you are not a threat, and they may even be willing to tell you how they succeed in doing it so well.

You will find that most of the examples quoted in this book are *not* industry-dependent. Even bankers should be able to relate to the *principles* of an innovative approach in the foundry or avionics business, and vice versa.

Notice also that something interesting happens when the seller–customer relationship is good, with the seller providing competitive product price performance as well as excellent customer-visible processes. *The customer becomes less and less inclined to make the product price performance comparisons.* This is another good reason for exploiting all opportunities to make your customer-visible processes excellent. (Of course, your product price performance must always be competitive, nevertheless.)

Invisible process excellence

The *invisible* business processes are just as important. They are the activities the customer does not normally see or directly experience. Examples of processes that are normally invisible are:

- 'select and certify suppliers'
- 'pay personnel'
- 'price products'
- 'educate and train personnel'
- 'manufacture products'.

Some of these invisible processes are necessary in order to create the product that is offered for sale. Others are needed simply to sustain the business. But they have to be excellent, too, relative to the competition. While the customer may not see or otherwise experience the invisible processes directly, the *results* of their performance *can* become visible, directly influencing the prices that the seller can sustain, for instance.

> **There is a saying, 'If the Japanese are not in your business, you are in the wrong business'. Mercedes has recently found it is in the *right* business.**
>
> **In 1992, its profits dropped 45 per cent and production costs were found to be 35 per cent higher than the relatively new Japanese competitors in its market segment. 1993 results were not better. That means that they had poor quality invisible business processes *relative to the competition*.**

Toyota, maker of the Lexus range of luxury cars, competing directly with Mercedes, has not stopped at making its invisible processes excellent. For its US customers, at least, it has invested in satellite communications systems and technology inside the car. For example, this allows a Lexus service agent to access that car's detailed service history, enabling speedy and effective repairs and service wherever the customer happens to be. This is very customer-visible.

A bad invisible process can have a negative impact on a process that *is* customer-visible. A poor quality 'educate and train personnel' process can result in hopelessly inadequate sales representatives doing a poor job of the highly visible process 'offer products for sale' even if the unfortunate sales representatives are offering products with superb price performance.

Invisible investments for quality, and competitiveness

A company in Belgium illustrates the importance of *invisible* process excellence. This company makes castings for bearings that are buried deep inside huge machines made by one of its customers, Caterpillar. The bearings themselves do not cost much, but the cost to Caterpillar (or its customers) can be very large if the machine breaks down because of a bearing failure.

This Belgian company differentiated itself from its competitors by making a very large investment in advanced testing equipment to check every single casting. Any flaw, and the castings go back in the pot to be melted down again. Thus, the company has invested heavily in the strategically important invisible process of monitoring product quality (it is strategically important both to the company and to an important customer, Caterpillar). The result is bearings for Caterpillar that have zero defects and a lot of business for the Belgian foundry.

The foundry has not neglected customer-visible processes, either. It is directly coupled to Caterpillar's procurement processes in order to support Just-In-Time delivery of its excellent products.

Vestra is a French clothing manufacturer. Its US subsidiary is Custom Vetment Associates. US retailers, such as Saks, have been given terminals for the French videotex system (Minitel).

A Saks tailor in New York can measure a customer for a bespoke suit, enter the details through the Minitel terminal, then send them via satellite to Vestra's main manufacturing operation at Strasbourg in France. An automated warehouse system presents the required cloth to a computer-controlled laser machine, which cuts out the suit. A staff of tailors does the finishing touches and the made-to-measure suit is shipped within four days. Contrast this with the old way, where the tailor had to order the cloth, wait for it, cut, assemble, and so on. Two or three months' wait was not unusual.

The Belgian foundry case may not qualify as an example of business re-engineering, but that of the French clothing manufacturer might fall within the '... radical re-design of business processes to achieve dramatic improvements in ...' part of our earlier definition. There, the customer-visible processes of the market-place are directly coupled across the Atlantic to the invisible processes involved in warehousing and manufacture.

Measuring Total Competitiveness

The phrase, 'if you can't measure it, you can't manage it' will be used from time to time in this book as a reminder of the importance of good measurements. We should begin by having an exact knowledge of the two factors that, when combined, give a measure of Total Competitiveness. At first, the measurement of your own Total Competitiveness will probably be less than exact, but, as the work described here proceeds, the precision will increase.

First, consider product price performance. For precision in this factor, the market-place must be segmented. For Kodak, for example, is it the product price performance of amateur roll film or of Kodak's optical scanning products, which can read documents at high speed and transform their contents into digital information, or is it X-ray film? This segmentation should be as detailed as you want it to be — by product, brand, product group, business unit, or whatever you choose. Then, ask the customer where you stand, compared with the competition, in terms of value for money — product price performance — on a scale of zero to 1.0, where 1.0 means the best. The segmentation means that a meaningful answer will

14

result, one that is revealing to management in the search for opportunities to improve Total Competitiveness.

Without segmentation, the required precision is missing. Imagine the buyer of amateur roll film being asked to assess the product price performance of Kodak as a whole. Some buyers of amateur roll film may well be buyers of Kodak's optical scanning products, but not many. An even smaller number will also be able to comment meaningfully on Kodak's X-ray film products.

For a company offering a portfolio of products to the same buyer — for example, financial services companies that offer a combination of retail banking, insurance, mortgages, and so on — there has to be a way of combining the component products to see how the portfolio compares as a whole. The method given below for combining customer-visible process qualities is one way of doing this.

Lists of customer-visible processes tend to be relatively longer than even those of segmented products or brands. There will only be one answer to the question related to product price performance if it is focused on only one product or brand, for example. However, it is difficult to imagine there being only one customer-visible process. There will be a different *set* of customer-visible processes depending on the chosen segmentation. The buyer of amateur roll film sees a different set of Kodak's customer-visible processes to those of the buyer of optical scanning equipment, though some will be the same.

To measure Total Competitiveness for the chosen market segmentation of product price performance, you need to know the relative customer satisfaction for the corresponding set of customer-visible processes, and this means *all* of them. For one particular segmentation, suppose the sample list of customer-visible processes quoted earlier is relevant, namely:

- 'bill customers'
- 'maintain/service installed products'
- 'deliver products'

- 'offer products for sale'
- 'advertise products'
- 'announce new products'.

Now the customer can be asked what is the quality of each of the customer-visible processes relative to the competition. Again, an answer of 1.0 means the process is the best. An answer of zero means the process is so bad, it cannot be compared. From the customer's point of view, it is a disaster — perhaps the 'deliver products' process for the customer in Helsinki, mentioned earlier.

For the chosen market segment, using Figure 1.1 as a means to display the information, all the customer-visible process qualities should be indicated along the horizontal axis. The poorest will then be clearly displayed. However, to calculate Total Competitiveness, we need a single number to describe the combined effects of customer-visible process excellence. Taking an average value is no good because it might conceal the fact that just *one* process is really terrible (like the 'deliver products' above) and, because of it, you lose the customer, despite the relative excellence of the rest of the package of qualities.

Suppose the responses to the questions for the above list of customer-visible processes are as follows:

Process	Relative excellence
'bill customers'	0.4
'maintain/service installed products'	1.0
'deliver products'	0.8
'offer products for sale'	1.0
'advertise products'	0.8
'announce new products'	0.6

The average here is 0.73, which is a fairly high score.

Suppose the product price performance is 1.0 — the best. Plotted on Figure 1.1, with such a high value for product price performance, the result is a large rectangle representing a deceptively high value for Total Competitiveness (1.0 × 0.73 = 0.73). This could, not unnaturally, create a feeling of well-being, even smugness. However, what about 'bill customers', with a relative quality of 0.4? Its potential for disaster has been hidden in the averaging process, but it is still highly visible to customers!

Now multiply the average by the score of the *worst* customer-visible process and a different picture emerges. The value of the customer-visible process component of Total Competitiveness now becomes 0.4 × 0.73 = 0.29. The corresponding Total Competitiveness is now 1.0 × 0.29 = 0.29. This is a tough test, but why not subject your enterprise to it? The idea is to *reveal* problems and opportunities, not to hide them. It also means that the truly awful process with a score of zero will still effectively reduce your Total Competitiveness to zero. This tends to attract the attention of senior management.

Now, suppose a major collective effort is made to ensure that the process 'bill customers' is relatively the best, from the customer's perspective. It now has a score of 1.0. The average customer-visible process score becomes 0.87. The worst process now is announcing new products, with a score of 0.6, so the customer-visible process factor to measure Total Competitiveness is 0.6 × 0.87 = 0.52. This is a big improvement on 0.29. Moreover, the management team knows where to focus next to maximize customer delight and competitor discomfort — the process with a score of 0.6, 'announce new products'.

This is a simplified example but illustrates the point. Process quality is not a static thing, so if you want to manage Total Competitiveness, you have to measure process quality continuously (some approaches to doing this are described in Chapter 19).

Clearly, the same approach can be applied to product price performance where there is a portfolio of products on offer to the same customer. Again, it highlights the need to do something dramatic (re-engineering?) about the worst ones, even though the average may be deceptively high.

Trapped by switching costs

The definition of Total Competitiveness includes nothing about so-called 'switching costs'. These are the costs of changing from one supplier to another, such as when re-writing computer systems, re-designing factory layouts, re-training personnel. They may be so high as to deter the customer from changing suppliers. From the perspective of the seller, switching costs may well appear to be an advantage. From the customer's perspective, they are a trap. Few, if any, customers will acknowledge switching costs as a competitive advantage. For this reason, and because Total Competitiveness is measured by *customers*, switching costs do not feature in the definition. Besides, innovative competitors will eventually find a way to release an imprisoned customer from captivity.

The definition of Total Competitiveness gets much of its value from its completeness. Fundamentally, there are only two kinds of business process — invisible and customer-visible.

It follows that everyone in the enterprise is working in either an invisible or a customer-visible process. There are no others. There is nowhere to hide. So, *everyone* in the enterprise is making a direct contribution, positive or negative, to Total Competitiveness.

Competitiveness is all about the excellence of business processes and their mutual internal dependencies. Business re-engineering is about quantum levels of transformation of a process or set of processes to competitive excellence. Some of the processes contribute directly to product price performance, others to creating and sustaining the win-win relationship with customers. All of them add costs and time.

The really critical opportunities — those that will have the biggest impact on Total Competitiveness — are found by taking a holistic view across *all* of the critical business processes, invisible and customer-visible. A holistic approach is what is described in this book. Such an approach is the only way the really important re-engineering and other opportunities will be found.

2

Total Effectiveness

Every principle and technique in this book can be also be applied to the non–commercial sector. There, the word 'competitiveness' is not usually appropriate because it implies choice. Normally, for example, you are stuck with the police force you have got. Even the United Kingdom's police force may become privatized one day, like other government agencies may be, but the 'client' will still have no choice. How *effective* is it, though, in comparison to the equivalent best–of–breed police force? Change a few words in the earlier definition and we have a definition of Total Effectiveness.

'Total Effectiveness' is the result of multiplying

1 **relative service cost performance and**
2 **relative client satisfaction with all "client-visible" business processes.**

'Relative' here means relative to the best-of-breed.

The first factor involves considering how well the services compare with the best supplier of police services, library services, tax collection, National Health Service hernia operations, or whatever, in terms of *what is provided and what it costs*. Price is not a consideration because the client normally has no choice, but you still have to pay. So, relative cost performance with what the best can do is important.

The second factor addresses the 'client-visible' processes, which are analogous to customer-visible processes. One day, the United Kingdom National Health Service might be able to provide the best cost performance in its hospitals in the world, but poor quality client-visible processes could prevent the right patients getting into these excellent hospitals. A police force can be cost-effective all right, but with surly, ill-mannered officers who alienate the general populace. This can have a detrimental effect on other police processes.

Things are changing: there is more of a focus on effectiveness from the client's point of view, and on costs. The once monolithic Civil Service in the UK has been broken into 92 free-standing agencies, each concentrating on a core function, such as administering teachers' pensions or repairing naval aircraft. Modelled on business, each agency is headed by a Chief Executive, who is responsible for achieving performance targets set by government ministers. Pay is linked to performance.

All is far from perfect yet, however. The report of the House of Commons Public Accounts Committee in January 1994 revealed an appalling catalogue of waste and mismanagement, with '... failings in ... key areas of financial control ... stewardship of public money and assets, and getting value for taxpayers' money'. Examples of such waste that were identified included the £66.5 million lost by the Property Services Agency because of a breakdown in invoicing. This suggests a terrible billing process. Then there was the £48 million spent by the Employment Department on a computer system, which was seen as poor value for money, as was the £11 million spent on '... haphazard consultants'. Wessex Health Authority spent £20 million on a computer system that never worked. A new accounting system at the Foreign Office '... created a climate which was conducive to fraud and theft.'

These are serious sums of money, as well as lost opportunities to the community. Maybe a focus on Total Effectiveness, such as is outlined in this book, might improve things?

Smiling with the tax collector

The Ontario Ministry of Revenue is addressing both factors simultaneously — cost performance and client satisfaction. It believes that by making it easier to pay taxes, it will collect more revenue, and at lower cost. There is a major focus on the quality of its client-visible processes. It wants them to be as good as those offered by the best hotels and banks. (This was described in *CSC Insights*, published by CSC Index, a company that specializes in re-engineering studies and implementation.)

The Ministry is giving corporate taxpayers electronic access to its information. With this access, it can send forms and collect tax electronically, faster and more cheaply. While retailers, for example, might lose two months' float of unpaid tax, they gain by not having forms to fill in and departments of people to do it. Less paperwork; less hassle. Win-win.

Instead of asking pensioners to fill in large and confusing forms every year, paying the huge cost of processing the forms, and answering the huge number of telephone queries, the Ministry looks at other internal systems to see if the pensioner's status has changed. If not, send the cheque. A hundred cheques per year may be incorrectly sent to dead people, but then the cheques cannot be cashed by anyone else.

In addition, an inward focus on invisible processes is improving relative cost-performance. The Ministry expects a five-year 40 per cent increase in workload, with no increase in personnel.

So, it can be done. Of course, it would be very difficult to maximize the Total Effectiveness of the United Kingdom's National Health Service, for example, by concentrating simultaneously on cost performance *and* on the excellence of client-visible processes, but it is also very difficult for a commercial enterprise to maximize, simultaneously, its product price performance *and* satisfaction with all its customer-visible processes. Nevertheless, you will find many examples in this book that show it *can* be done. The challenge is the same. In the one case, top management has a duty to the community to get it right. This means maximizing Total Effectiveness. In the other, the duty is to the owners of the business. This means maximizing Total Competitiveness. In both situations, the key is to focus on the most critical business processes. This is precisely the focus of business re-engineering. (From this point on, 'competitiveness' will be used to mean 'competitiveness or effectiveness', and 'customers' for 'customers or clients'.)

Part 2

FINDING THE OPPORTUNITIES FOR COMPETITIVENESS

3

Seven questions that need answers

'Strategic management is rather like making love. You cannot delegate it.
You can read books and manuals about it, study videos, even employ consultants. But if want to get it right, you have to do it yourself.'

Professor Charles–Hubert Haevart, University of Leuven, Belgium.

Here are seven simple questions.

1 What is the future desired state of the enterprise?

2 What are its Critical Success Factors?

3 What are its most critical business processes?

4 What is the future desired state of each critical process?

5 What are the inputs needed by each critical process?

6 Who are the suppliers of necessary inputs?

7 What is the most competitive structure of each critical process?

These questions are deceptively simple. In fact, they are fundamental. And they are free of jargon and trendy academic words, or fashionable phrases from some eminent management shaman. ('Critical Success Factor' is a bit modern, I suppose, having first appeared in the *Harvard Business Review* as recently as 1961 in 'Management Information Crisis', by D. R. Daniel.) The questions are as down-to-earth and basic as the techniques described later.

A visitor from outer space could be excused for believing that every senior manager on earth could answer all of them immediately. The fact that managers *cannot* readily answer them is the justification for this book.

Their simplicity belies their power. Answer them, and you will discover what is necessary to maximize your Total Competitiveness. Implementation has to follow, of course, and this will probably mean re-engineering. (Detailed considerations of implementation, however, are outside the scope of this book. Here, we are largely concerned with finding the most important opportunities.)

The seven questions can only be answered by the top-management team (these are strategic issues, so they cannot be delegated). It normally takes two to three days of hard work, after Question 1 has been answered. The working days need not be contiguous, though the interval should not be longer than four weeks or so.

Imagine that the questions are linked by a thread that cannot be broken. The answers to one question are the prerequisites for the next one. The sequence cannot be changed, nor can questions be skipped.

Seven timeless questions

Not only are the questions simple, they are timeless. The people who built the European railway network in the nineteenth century would have understood them. Equally, they will need to be answered by any top management team a hundred years from now. Implementation will be dramatically different then, though, and heaven knows what kind of technology will be available, or what will be the political and social environment — compare today with a hundred years ago! The term re-engineering may even have vanished utterly in a hundred years. Whatever happens, though, people will still need the answers to these seven perfectly reasonable questions, regardless of industry, regardless of any labels or management terminology of the time.

The precision with which a top management team knows the answers today is a measure of its fitness to run the enterprise on behalf of its owners or the community.

---

1   What is the future desired state of the enterprise?

This might be equated to the single word, 'mission'. The trouble is that the English language is too rich in near-synonyms of the word mission. One person's mission is another's goals or aims or objectives or even vision statement. (I am still waiting for the word 'quest' to appear in the literature. It will.) Even in the same management journal, such words are used interchangeably.

To avoid ambiguity, I use the phrase 'future desired state'. This is a brief, unambiguous description of what the enterprise should look like in two, three, maybe five years time — whatever is the strategic timeframe.

It is the top management team's responsibility, *together*, to take the enterprise from its condition today to its future desired state.

---

2   What are the critical success factors?

These are the management team's views of what are the most important things, things that must be accomplished to ensure the future desired state of the enterprise. Each Critical Success Factor is, therefore, by definition, *necessary*; together they are *sufficient* to accomplish the future desired state. There will normally be between five and an absolute maximum of eight of them. Clearly, these cannot be decided until there is a precise description of the future desired state of the enterprise.

It is not appropriate that Critical Success Factors have individual ownership. They are jointly owned — like the enterprise's future desired state — by the top management team that creates them.

---

3 What are the most critical business processes?

These are the business processes that need to be of excellent quality in order to accomplish the Critical Success Factors. Moreover, each critical process *must* have an executive owner, a member of the top-management team that is responsible for the enterprise's future desired state, (and has just agreed the Critical Success Factors). So, it is a short and rather exclusive list of business processes.

Critical business processes tend to be cross-functional in scope. Subprocesses tend to be in a department or function. A focus on one or more subprocesses without there being a responsibility and accountability for the entire process is not enough. This is because once a transaction or input enters the process, it can vanish; nobody knows where it is until it appears at the other end. All the time it is adding cost, the potential for customer dissatisfaction and other opportunities to get it wrong, a common problem with 'bill customers'.

---

4 What is the future desired state of each process?

These are the descriptions of competitive excellence for each critical business process. Rarely, if ever, does a process future desired state description correspond with the process quality as it is today.

Now we are at the stage where the future desired state of the enterprise has been broken down into a manageable number of *business process* future desired states, and each has an executive owner.

> **5 What inputs are needed by each process?**
>
> At the top management level, most of the necessary inputs to achieve process excellence are in the form of information. Each process owner must decide what information — and anything else — will be needed to improve the process from its current quality to the competitive excellence of its future desired state.
>
> **6 Who are the suppliers of necessary inputs?**
>
> Knowing the necessary inputs, each process owner must then identify the corresponding sources of supply. Most of the suppliers will be colleagues in the top-management team — fellow owners of critical business processes. Other sources of supply will be beyond the enterprise's boundary — external suppliers.

Knowing the answers to the first six questions, a complete internal model of the enterprise can be made, showing every supplier-to-process-to-customer relationship (internal customer, that is), for the most critical business processes. One more question needs to be answered, though, before projects to maximize Total Competitiveness — the re-engineering and other projects — should be specified and put in place.

> **7 What should be the competitive structure of each process?**
>
> This asks where each process will be performed. If it is in more than one place, a second question becomes necessary: what is the degree of internal coupling (that is, the degree of coordination *inside* the process) needed to maximize its competitive impact? This can range from zero — total autonomy at each location — to 100 per cent, when the process is so strongly coupled, all locations perform as though they were one.

Now the Total Competitiveness projects can be defined and prioritized. The technologies of the day can be exploited. But the questions themselves are timeless.

Today's technology for connecting process to process is telecommunications. Telecommunications also provides the internal coupling between locations *within* each process.

The top management of the Roman Empire did not have electronics to help them couple their business processes. Instead, they made strategic investments in roads to provide the necessary information flows, as well as for the movement of troops and goods. Some processes were very strongly controlled from a regional centre, in Gaul, say. Some were delegated to a more local 'business unit general manager', say, in Verulamium (modern day St Albans, in England). Others were strongly coordinated and controlled from the corporate headquarters in Rome.

With their good processes and good communications, it was probably as fast to get a very urgent message from Corstopitum, close to the Roman Wall in Northern England, to Rome in AD 400 as by surface mail from modern-day Corbridge today. (I have just received some Christmas cards at my home in France that were posted in England on 14 December. Today is 17 January. This is far from a unique case.) For *very* urgent communication, the Romans could use beacons: not much content in the message, but speeds of hundreds of miles per hour could be achieved.

The Romans understood Total Competitiveness, but they did not need to define it. Their invisible and client-visible processes were excellent, sustained by the universal Roman Law, engineering standards, and so forth. They had excellent communications, relative to the competition. They were thereby able to manage a rich and expanding 'global' enterprise against strong competition for over 400 years. That the processes and communications eventually collapsed and the competition moved in was due to the corrupt nature of the top management, their seeking of favours and the purchasing of high office. The job title became more important than the job. There are lessons in this for us today.

4
The members of the study team

These should be the boss and the boss's immediate management team — nobody else. But the boss of what?

Given the word 'enterprise' has been used in this book to cover commercial and non-commercial organizations, the boss could be the:

- owner of a chain of shops
- Corporate or Group Chief Executive
- Prime Minister
- Director of a hospital
- CEO of a Civil Service Agency
- Managing Director of a business unit
- Divisional Chief Executive
- Managing Director of a company
- Director of a research laboratory
- Chief Officer of a city
- Senior Partner of a consultancy
- Chief Executive of a subsidiary, and so forth.

A real or imaginary boundary can be drawn around the enterprise and the boss can say, 'This piece is mine'. It can be anything from a global corporation to a hospital or a company's education and training centre.

A common factor in all of these is the existence of a person at the top who has responsibility across the entire scope of the enterprise concerned. This person does not have a specific *functional* responsibility, such as marketing, psychiatry, finance, housing, sales or whatever. Members of the boss's top-management team usually have such responsibilities — at least, when the study starts. At the end, they may be different.

It is assumed that the boss is appointed to do something rather more strenuous than 'minding the shop', and that the job is too difficult to do alone, so the boss has a management team to help. This team normally numbers between five and, say, a dozen people.

These (and the boss) are the participants in the study. They have the collective responsibility of taking the enterprise from its condition today to its future desired state.

It is also assumed that the future desired state is not one of extinction, even though a variant of the technique can be used to manage the elegant departure of a business unit from the world, for example. Here, the underlying assumption is that the enterprise needs to become more competitive/effective and wants to succeed.

The boss invites the team to attend. All members (including the boss) must be present at all times. No substitutes should be allowed, and no 'assistants' or other hitchhikers — just the top management team.

I ran a one-day session with the President of IBM Spain and his team. It was early December and the country sales quota had not quite been achieved, yet. The Vice-President of Marketing protested that he could not possibly attend. The President insisted, and he attended, grudgingly, because he was given no choice. At the end of the session, he said to me, 'You were absolutely right to insist on us all being here. It could not possibly have worked otherwise.'

The country sales quota was achieved.

If all members of the team cannot be present, don't do it. *All* members, at every stage, have to buy in to the process if it is to succeed.

An external facilitator is useful. The task of the facilitator is to ask the questions and insist on clear, unambiguous answers. A good facilitator will draw the responses from the participants and not make direct contributions. After all, the participants are assumed to be the best-qualified group of people to do the job of achieving the future desired state. The facilitator must also maintain the impetus of the work, while insisting on unanimity at all stages. Getting the boss to rule on a contentious issue is a cop-out.

How to fail

1 Do it with a member of the team missing for part or all of the time.

This is an intense, hard-working, team-building effort. The missing member is liable to say, at a later date, 'I would never have agreed to that. It's crazy!', or some such.

2 Do it with a newly appointed boss.

The new boss should have been in the job long enough to know the job and the team well enough to work together — three months, perhaps?

3 Do it with a boss who is about to leave.

A waste of time and money. Wait until the new boss is appointed, then see 2, above.

4 Do it with a dictatorial boss.

If the boss cannot tolerate participation and rejects contributions from members of the team, don't do it. At the end, the boss may not like what has emerged and is liable to say, 'Very interesting session, but I have decided this is what we are going to do anyway.'

5 Expect to preserve the status quo.

If you start with the assumption that you have got it right, don't do it. There is no guarantee that everyone will like what emerges, but it will be right. Be prepared for surprises and embrace them as opportunities.

6 Do it in the boardroom.

Get off site and leave the fielding of telephone calls to someone outside of your enterprise. If you do the work on your own premises, secretaries will manage to borrow a thermic lance from somewhere and cut holes in concrete walls!

Part 3

ANSWERING THE SEVEN KEY QUESTIONS

5

The future desired state of the enterprise

The thread that links the seven questions starts here. When any difficult issue arises regarding the subsequent analysis, come directly back to the future desired state of the enterprise. This is the ultimate starting point, the standard against which to measure the relevance of all future discussion, so it has got to be right.

Our traveller from outer space might assume that every top-management team would *at least* know the answer to this question in order to have a clear understanding of what they are collectively trying to do with the enterprise. Not so.

A top-management team has a varying population, including the boss. People are appointed, stay a while, do their jobs, and move on. There are long-serving members, and newer arrivals.

The individual team members know their individual jobs — outstandingly well, usually. At least in well-run enterprises, the new Director of Marketing or Surgery, for example, has a clear job description and an equally clear understanding of the remuneration package. The job tends to be inherited from the predecessor, along with the office, the furniture, the systems, the habits, and so on.

Even in well-run enterprises, however, there is usually only the vaguest idea about what is its *specific* overall purpose. There will be a feeling that it should make profits or heal people, for example, but only rarely is there a clear statement about where it should be heading as a whole.

The focus often tends to be on individual functional or departmental excellence, with correspondingly clear departmental or functional goals. In any case, this is how the remuneration package tends to work. The collective responsibility of the top management team to accomplish something specific is rarely articulated, however. It is this *collective* responsibility that is described in the future desired state.

Portentous statements abound, it is true, in annual reports, internal communications, press releases, and so forth. Often they are larded with motherhood statements and declarations about them being 'a caring employer' or phrases like 'a good corporate citizen' — you can almost hear the soft music. These are all right in their place, but not much good for moving the business forward, which is the job of the top-management team. Typically, such statements are rather insubstantial declarations about how marvellous the enterprise *is*. They don't describe how good it *should be*. But often, this is *all* there is. Rarely will you see a clear, unambiguous statement describing exactly where the enterprise must be in two or three years' time. A well-known and very direct one that *did* say something definite about its future desired state is from the Japanese earth-moving equipment manufacturer, Komatsu. It said simply: 'We will encircle Caterpillar'. Everybody knew where *they* were going.

Here is a statement of the future desired state made by one of my clients, a UK supermarket company: 'We shall survive until this time next year'.

This is pretty direct and measurable. In a year's time, the company either exists or it does not. (The Board then went on to agree the Critical Success Factors for its survival, and identified the most critical business processes to ensure it.)

This is an extreme case. The company concerned was a family-owned business and it had twelve difficult months to negotiate, without prejudicing the value of the business. The future desired state was very near-term, tactically focused. They succeeded. At the end of the year, the family sold the business for what they regarded as a decent price.

In 1993, the UK's Midland Bank's mission was: 'To become Britain's most recommended bank by 1995'.

This future desired state is very much oriented towards customers, and prospective customers. Notice that it says nothing about profits. To become Britain's most *profitable* bank by 1995 would be a totally different mission, with totally different Critical Success Factors, and a correspondingly different set of critical business processes.

Here, the strategic intent is to enlarge the bank's customer base. Good profits will follow if the customer–acquisition processes are supported by excellent customer–retention processes, of course, and efficient (cost–competitive) internal, invisible processes. Clearly, these processes must also *exist* today, to sustain the business, but the principal focus in the near term must be on the bank's reputation, *from the customer's perspective*, regarding the bank's customer–visible business processes. *They* must be the priority processes for resources and for management attention.

The desired state, not the means

Notice that these three brief examples — Komatsu, the supermarket company, and Midland Bank — describe only the future desired state, not the means of accomplishing it. This is how it should be. The future desired state of a newly elected prime minister might be the equally short, 'we get re-elected'.

Here is another one. This dates from 1987 and was the mission of IBM's European International Education Centre, in Belgium.

> **'Prepare IBM World Trade Europe, Middle East, Africa Corporation employees to establish their businesses.**
>
> **Organize high-level seminars for IBM customers and make a significant contribution to IBM's image in Europe.**
>
> **Demonstrate the added value of the International Education Centre through excellence in advanced education, internationalism, innovation, and cross-functional exchanges.'**

This is good, in parts.

On the good side, it defines the boundaries of the enterprise — IBM's Europe, Middle East, Africa Corporation. It also defines its market-place: the Centre's customer population is all IBM employees within that area, plus senior people from IBM's customers. It says what has to be done: prepare IBM employees, make a significant contribution to IBM's image in Europe, and demonstrate the added value of the Education Centre. These can be measured.

On the bad side, it also contains the *means* of doing it, by organizing '... high-level seminars for IBM customers ... excellence in advanced education, internationalism, innovation, and cross-functional exchanges'. These phrases are not only redundant in a description of an enterprise's future desired state, they also lock the management team into a way of doing things — the old way. It may still turn out to be the *best* way, of course, but it is harder to challenge the status quo if the means are embedded in its future desired state. It is vital to keep the *what* — the future desired state — separate from the *how* — the means of achieving it.

A similar mixture of the *what* and the *how* is evident in the mission of IBM UK in 1993.

> **'IBM UK will be the leader in applying advanced information technology and expertise to answer our customers' needs.**
>
> **We will build long-term relationships in a profitable and caring manner to assure continuing value in what we provide.**
>
> **It is the way we put together the best skills and technology that sets us apart.'**

The first sentence is the *what* — the future desired state. It is all that is needed. The second two sentences are part of the *how*. This is not nit-picking. It is easy to imagine the top management of IBM UK protesting that, 'it is *obvious* that we must build long-term relationships, ... , etc.', and, ' ... of *course* we will set ourselves apart by the way we put together the best skills and technology!' Maybe. But we assume that *nothing* is obvious. If it *is* obvious, the ensuing analysis will reveal it, in addition to some surprises. Remember, the thread starts here. All aspects of the status quo are to be challenged from this point on.

Creating a description of the future desired state means getting just that — not the *means* of doing it. *Finding the means is the whole point.* This is where the re-engineering and other opportunities will be found, and there will always be those valuable surprises.

Creating the future desired state

The preferred way of preparing for the two to three days of collective effort is for the boss to spend some time beforehand preparing a view of the future desired state; a first cut, if you like. If you start with a management team and a blank sheet of paper, endless time can be spent together on the gestation of an agreed future desired state.

The boss should have a good idea of what the enterprise should look like in the future, being privileged not only by virtue of seniority, but also by having an across-the-board view. It does not matter if the boss spends a number of weeks ruminating over it. If the study opens with an obviously well thought-out statement, the hard, collective work of the study can start quickly. Normally, up to about two hours can be allowed to discuss, modify, and agree the final wording of the future desired state. This participation by all team members should be encouraged. It can be very revealing. Quite early into the discussion with the Board of a large tobacco company, the CEO said, 'It is rapidly becoming clear to me that I have not been doing my job properly. You don't seem to understand what we should be doing with the business and I have not properly understood your problems.' Such humility, though, is rare. Eventually, after not more than two hours of discussion, the boss may have to step in and say, 'Enough. This is now our Future Desired State.' It is the *only* time when the boss should pull rank, and has only very rarely been necessary, in my experience.

This all tends to be rather more difficult for non-commercial enterprises. They usually do not have even vague 'mission' statements. A technique that worked well with the management team of the city of Winchester, in England, was as follows.

During a brief brainstorming session one evening, key words were collected from the team regarding the theme of what they thought they should be doing for the community — collectively. Then they went home with the list of words and thought about it. Next day, it took about two hours to get a really crisp future desired state description.

They were delighted because then they could go forward.

During the afternoon, the Chief Executive drew me to one side and said, 'It's beginning to work. Have you noticed how they have started to say *"we"* instead of *"I"*?'

Another useful approach is to start from a generic future desired state, such as 'we shall maximize the Total Effectiveness of the enterprise' (this would obviously be for a non-commercial enterprise because of the word 'effectiveness'). Maximizing Total Effectiveness may then be viewed as the overall framework within which to create a more situation-specific future desired state. For example, one particular region of the UK's National Health Service must have the worst mortality statistics in the country, *relative to the other regions* (they are not all the same; one of them has to be the worst). When the question, 'What exactly do we *mean* by "Total Effectiveness"?' is asked, the managers might frame a

44

region-specific future desired state that says: 'The mortality rate in this region will improve at a faster year–on–year rate than the average for the UK.'

The other regions are presumably trying to improve *their* mortality rates, too, but this region is statistically behind them all. The above future desired state, if accomplished, would ensure that the region moves from the bottom of the list in terms of mortality rate. This puts the main focus on that part of the population which is dying relatively earlier (everybody does it eventually!) and thereby making the region bottom of the league. It defines the target population for health care — both preventive and curative — that will have the biggest impact on mortality statistics and, thereby, on the agreed future desired state.

I do not mean to suggest that this is the correct future desired state for this region, of course, but *somebody* has to decide, and it is not the job of any external consultant.

A different set of Critical Success Factors would result, and a correspondingly different set of critical business processes, if the management team should decide instead to have a description of the future desired state that runs along the lines of: 'The general health of the population in this region will improve on a year–on–year basis at a faster rate than the average for the United Kingdom.'

This future desired state is saying that, on average, *everyone* in the region will get healthier. *Everyone* is the target.

In contrast, the future desired state that is focused on relative mortality rates recognizes that many people in this region already *are* healthy, aware of health matters like smoking, stress, exercise, alcohol and drug abuse, and so on, and that they will *remain* healthy. The healthy people can't be ignored, of course, particularly when it comes to *curing* people, but the main focus will be on the target population that is *not* so aware, and which is dying relatively earlier than in other regions.

45

Again, a completely different result will follow if the future desired state reflects a view that the National Health Service exists only to *cure* people who need medical care. It could then be described as the National Healing Service. The *general* health of the client population would then be outside the bounds of its future desired state. Presumably, some other enterprise would have to do that, with a correspondingly different set of Critical Success Factors and critical business processes.

A commercial organization can also sometimes find it useful to start from the generic 'We shall maximize our Total Competitiveness', then go on to something company-specific. This approach was used to create the following future desired state for a UK company. Assume it is January 1993.

'By end 1996, we will:

- **hold relative market share versus Woodhouses and C. J. Barton**
- **be perceived by consumers as being the best place to shop for ladies' fashion items**
- **financially outperform Woodhouses and C. J. Barton.'**

(The only changes made to this statement are those necessary to preserve the anonymity of the company.)

There is no waffle or cant in this statement; no top management sloganeering. It is explicitly focused on the main competitors of the company — Woodhouses and C. J. Barton — with regard to its statements about market share and the relative efficiency of running the business.

It is focused on the customers, too, because it states in what respect the company will be acknowledged to be the best, namely in ladies' fashion items. The company may very effectively sell a much wider product range, but it plans to be renowned for excellence in ladies' fashion items. It is medium-term in scope — four years — and it will effectively equip the company to move forward *after* 1996.

An imaginary UK retail organization will be used to illustrate how to answer the seven key questions. A real company could not be used — too much would be revealed. Nevertheless, it is based on a real company, but heavily disguised.

Doppler Electronics

Doppler is a large part of a rather diversified group with head-quarters in London. Total sales in 1993 were £4.3 billion (about $6.7 billion). The group plans to expand by means of selective acquisition and strategic alliances to exploit the opportunities of the post-1992 Single European Market.

The Group's CEO is also the CEO of Doppler. He prepared for the Doppler study by working with the Group's Board to define the future desired state of the entire Group. This formed the basis for defining the first draft of a future desired state for Doppler. This was debated, modified, and agreed by Doppler's Board. Every member bought in to it.

Keeping to the spirit and the title of this book, we shall use Doppler's generic future desired state to illustrate the technique:

'We shall maximize the Total Competitiveness of Doppler Electronics.'

No real-life organization should use such a generic future desired state. Indeed, you are strongly recommended to create a more enterprise-specific future desired state. It will give much sharper focus to the process of identifying your Critical Success Factors, and all the subsequent analysis. After all, the future desired state is the starting point of the thread that will lead to identifying the strategic re-engineering opportunities, and other ways of becoming more competitive.

A good future desired state should always describe a state of improved Total Competitiveness/Effectiveness, however. In the case of the UK retailer of ladies fashion items referred to earlier, it describes a state of improved Total Competitiveness that is focused on C. J. Barton and Woodhouses. In the case of the National Health Service region, it will be improved Total Effectiveness, but focused *either* on mortality rate *or* on the general health of all of the population in the region, whichever is chosen.

Armed with a clear definition of where they are going, the management team of Doppler Electronics can now identify what is necessary to get there — the Critical Success Factors.

6

The Critical Success Factors

Doppler's top management team have agreed exactly what they are trying to do with the enterprise — moving it towards its future desired state. This is the prerequisite for agreeing those critical things at which they must be spectacularly successful if they are to be confident about achieving the future desired state. *These* are the Critical Success Factors.

The agreed set of Critical Success Factors has two vital characteristics:

- each Critical Success Factor is *necessary*
- together, they are *sufficient*.

Together, they represent the irreducible minimum of essentials that must be achieved in order to accomplish the future desired state of the enterprise.

The necessity and sufficiency condition must be satisfied.

Critical Success Factors have something in common with your heart, brain, lungs, digestive system, and so on: you can't do without any one of them, you can't prioritize them. It is meaningless to ask me whether I would prefer to lose my brain or my heart because I need *both*. There are many other parts that you could remove from the inside as well as from the outside of me, though, without which I could still continue as a viable Maurice Hardaker (I would rather they were *not* removed, of course), but take away one of the critical bits and I effectively cease to exist.

It is at a comparably visceral level that Critical Success Factors should be defined.

The absolute maximum number of Critical Success Factors is eight. There is a sort of justification for the number eight in that some research showed that the human brain cannot simultaneously handle more than between about five and eight different things at the same time. However, the *real* reason is that if you do not impose quite a small limit, the focus becomes diffuse and it is difficult to stop adding to the list. You can end up with a long list of problems and moans rather than a sharply focused list of what has to be achieved.

Critical Success Factors have to be agreed by the top-management team. Typically, they begin with phrases like, 'we must' or 'we need'. That it is a collectively agreed requirement is evidenced by the words 'we' or 'our'. That the factor is of imperative necessity is expressed by words like 'must' or 'need'. And the exact wording must be agreed by all. This is not a thing for voting, nor should it be left to the boss to decide.

It takes time, particularly for the first two or three Critical Success Factors. I normally find that a management team can agree them in a morning, after perhaps an hour's discussion on the future desired state, but it can take a whole hour to get just the first two agreed. Then it accelerates. People learn how to think in Critical Success Factor terms.

Use strong language

First, Critical Success Factors should not be 'vanilla flavoured'. It is easy to say 'We must have skilled personnel'. It certainly seems to be a reasonable candidate for becoming one of the Critical Success Factors, and it turns up often.

But surely there are skilled personnel in the enterprise today? Which *particular* skills will be critically needed to accomplish the future desired state? Marketing people? Neurosurgeons? Financial wizards? Diplomats? Environmentalists? What is it about the resource 'skills' that is missing or deficient, and which is necessary to accomplish the future desired state? What is it about the resource 'skills' that will differentiate the enterprise from its competitors? You may reasonably assume that *they* will create a vanilla–flavoured Critical Success Factor 'We must have skilled personnel' — most people do — but here is your chance to get ahead.

Some time ago, I did a study with the Board of a large brewing company in the UK. Over the previous 250 years or so, it had acquired 48 breweries and about 4500 pubs, the traditional outlet for its products. The 'manufacturing' strategy was to close down the old 48 breweries and build three huge plants, rather like oil refineries. What they lacked in rustic charm they made up for in efficiency, measured in cost performance.

Their fourth Critical Success Factor was: 'We must develop and optimize non-traditional outlets for our products'.

You can sell only a certain amount of beer in 4500 pubs. Most of the rest of the pubs were owned by competitors, which made it difficult to acquire more of them. So it was necessary to develop and optimize non-traditional outlets for their products. Otherwise, their three, new, gigantic breweries would run at less than optimum capacity. Up would go the costs. So, they had to find other ways in which to get rid of the stuff — golf clubs, squash clubs, airlines, supermarkets, whatever.

Their declared business strategy was one of aggressive expansion. The Group CEO looked hard at this fourth Critical Success Factor. Then he said, 'I've just realized that our strategy is *not* one of aggressive expansion. We are moving into retailing. And we don't know anything about retailing!'

Within ten seconds, Critical Success Factor 5 had been proposed and agreed. It said: 'We must acquire retailing skills'.

It was a strategic necessity.

There are other kinds of blandly flavoured Critical Success Factors. 'We must have premises in which to work' is an extreme example, just to illustrate the point. Of *course* you must have premises. You cannot be expected to run a modern business in the woods, in the rain. But if your premises are so run down, unhealthy, and dangerous that the Government will close your business down (or the employees will leave — there go your skills), then a Critical Success Factor focused on the need to secure *better* premises becomes valid. Better premises are as critical to survival as are the heart, lungs, and so forth. If you already have suitable premises, however, it is stating the obvious to say that you need them. Beware of wasting opportunities this way — you can not have more than eight, after all.

Strong adjectives and adverbs are appropriate in Critical Success Factors. If you really believe, 'We must have the finest marketing skills in Europe' is a necessary condition for accomplishing your future desired state, then say so. Not to say it is to duck the issue. And you will never get the skills. Nor will you ever achieve the future desired state.

Make them strategic

Critical Success Factors should express a strategic rather than a tactical need. They are relatively long-term; long enough that you can reasonably expect an effective management team to have set in place the often quite large investments and other changes needed to achieve them. Along with the future desired state (from which they are derived), they are the ultimate source of re-engineering opportunities, which will be identified later.

So, a statement such as, 'We must regain J. W. Scranton as a customer by the end of next month' cannot be used as a Critical Success Factor. If it is, nevertheless, very important to the business, perhaps it should be a short-term goal for the person in charge of marketing, or even the Chief Executive. If it is critical to the survival of the business, then stop the study, focus all management attention on regaining the lost customer, then start again.

On the other hand, Critical Success Factors do not last for ever. I normally recommend that the management team revisits its list after a year or so. Sometimes, quite small (though necessary) changes result. Then, the impact of the *changes* on last year's answers to the subsequent questions must be assessed. This ensures that the enterprise can be kept constantly in tune with whatever the management team believes can impact its future desired state.

Equally, if there are dramatic changes in the business environment (a merger or takeover, a powerful new competitor appears, new legislation, new market opportunities, for example) then you should review the impact of the changes on your answers to all seven questions as soon as possible. The appointment of a new chief executive can result in quite dramatic changes. At Midland Bank, for example, in December 1993, it was announced that the CEO, Brian Pearse, would be replaced by Keith Whitson, an old hand at the parent bank, Hong Kong and Shanghai Banking Corporation. Moreover, the Midland's Chairman, Sir Peter Walters, would be replaced by the driving force of the Hong Kong and Shanghai Banking Corporation, Sir William Purves. People at Midland should not expect the old status quo to be preserved in these circumstances.

Make them enterprise-specific

The more your Critical Success Factors are specific to your enterprise at the time they are decided, the better. Yet, people often propose something as a Critical Success Factor that is totally outside their sphere of influence.

During a time of very high interest rates, the following was proposed by the Board of a large UK company in the wine business: 'We must have lower interest rates'.

The members of the Board were vehement in defending this as a Critical Success Factor. They all agreed that it was critical to the future health and success of the business. Yet, as a Board of Directors, they could have no direct influence on interest rates. When I asked, 'What is it about high interest rates that is hurting your business?', there was a long silence. Then one Director said, slowly, 'I

> think I can see what he's getting at. He's talking about inventory levels. Financing our high inventory levels is what is costing us so much because of the high cost of money. We can insulate ourselves from the effects of high interest rates if we reduce our inventory levels!'
>
> The *real* Critical Success Factor that emerged quite quickly was along the lines of: 'We must dramatically reduce our inventory levels by ... (date)'.

(It has to be said that *I* was not talking about inventory levels, by the way. I just wanted to know what the company-specific difficulty was. I did not know. But the Board knew. They just had to find the right words. *Then* they could do something about it.)

Another example that illustrates this point is one which often appears: 'We must increase market share'.

True, this would be wonderful to achieve, particularly as it will usually be at the expense of competitors. But try to make it more specific to *your* enterprise in *its* industry and *its* environment. For a company in the avionics business, for example, the more company-specific expression of this Critical Success Factor might be: 'We must become a preferred supplier to Airbus Industries by ... (date)'.

This would provide a much sharper focus for all members of the top-management team (not just the people in sales and marketing), and it provides a much clearer framework for identifying the business processes whose excellence will be necessary to accomplish it. After all, re-engineering investments are applied to business processes, not to Critical Success Factors.

> It is easy to imagine an enterprise-specific Critical Success Factor for a company in Belgium that was bought by a Finnish company from a US-based multinational. For over a year, all of the new Finnish subsidiary's financial and customer processing was done through a telecommunications link to a competitor's computer in the United States. It was that of the original owners of the business.

Another very important point. Do not repeat any part of the future desired state in your list of Critical Success Factors. The future desired state might contain something like, ' . . . and become the dominant supplier of confectionery products in Spain'. Then to go on and create a Critical Success Factor that says 'We must become the dominant supplier of confectionery products in Spain' is useless. This is just going round in circles. What has to be defined is precisely *what is necessary to become* the dominant supplier of confectionery products in Spain. It may be necessary to have two or three Critical Success Factor statements to describe how to make this happen. Remember that the Critical Success Factors are statements of what is necessary and sufficient to accomplish the future desired state, so repetition is not helpful.

Make them pure

Beware of using the word 'and' in a Critical Success Factor. It is tempting after a lot of hard work, and with nine of them on the wall to say, 'Let's combine numbers two and seven to say, "We must reduce total delivered costs of our products and improve employee morale" '. It gets the total down to eight, certainly, but the result is a statement that is not a Critical Success Factor. It is too diffuse. Critical Success Factors should have an elemental purity about them, like hydrogen, or lithium, germanium, gold.

(Looking ahead to the next question, 'What are the most critical business processes?' provides another reason for avoiding the word 'and'. When we address this question, we shall be finding out which business processes have to exist *and* be excellent to accomplish each individual Critical Success Factor. It is obvious that a different set of processes will have to be excellent to reduce total delivered costs compared with those needed to improve morale. They may even be in conflict. 'And' in a Critical Success Factor is all right so long as it is collecting *similar* things together, consistent with what has been said above. But beware of it.)

In the above example, reducing the number of Critical Success Factors from nine to eight might be a hard slog, but it has to be done. It should not be beyond the capability of the best paid, most experienced, and most senior people in the enterprise to agree the no more than eight things that must be done outstandingly well to move their enterprise forward to its future desired state.

The Doppler Electronics team started identifying their Critical Success Factors on the morning of the first day of their study. The following list was agreed by lunchtime. These Critical Success Factors would then be used to find their most critical processes.

Doppler Electronics' Critical Success Factors

1 Each customer must perceive ours to be a superior product range.
2 We must convince consumers that we offer a superior level of service.
3 We must win consumer acceptance that our pricing is fully competitive with industry leaders.
4 Each store must substantially achieve its optimum performance.
5 We must give to the stores the support they need for the business to achieve its objectives.
6 We must enable/empower our people to perform to their full potential.
7 We must establish relationships with key suppliers, to the disadvantage of our competitors.
8 We must grow Doppler's operating profit by at least 20 per cent per year.

You may not like or even approve of the Doppler management team's view of their Critical Success Factors. It does not matter. *They* regarded them as being necessary and sufficient. *They* are the best-qualified people on earth to decide them. In the same way, *your* top-management team is the best-qualified group of people to decide *your* Critical Success Factors. And you should never allow anyone to tell you they are wrong.

Table 6.1 Some examples of Critical Success Factors

These are all real-world Critical Success Factors from a wide variety of industries. They are provided to help you in the formulation of your own Critical Success Factors.

We must deliver zero defect products that never fail in service.

This is from a medical products company. It could equally well come from a company in the avionics industry, or many others.

We must be better at selecting the winners from our bucket of ideas.

This company was brimming with great ideas for new products, but it had not always chosen the best ones to commercialize.

We must find the means to decrease unemployment in the city of Plymouth.

Competitiveness is a concept that is clearly understood in some parts of the non-commercial sector. Here, the Chief Officer and his team were looking to compete with other cities to attract new industry, in order to reduce unemployment in Plymouth.

Next is a related CSF from the City of The Hague, in Holland.

We must provide education facilities that match the needs of our target businesses.

The Hague's target businesses were the quiet, pollution-free high-technology ones, and financial services (not heavy industry). The management team saw The Hague as competing with other cities in Europe to attract them. Appropriate education facilities were regarded as critical to attract the senior people in their target businesses.

We must secure reliable, high-quality suppliers.

From a company moving to Just-In-Time manufacturing. (This Critical Success Factor really could have been made a lot stronger by phrasing it in such a way as to differentiate the company more from its competitors.)

We must improve and retain the quality of our human resources.

The word 'and' is acceptable here — the processes of improving and retaining are sufficiently related to one aim.

We must have the most superb distribution system in our industry.

From a bank. This is very aggressive, but it is what the team believed.

We need a much clearer understanding of market opportunities and requirements.

Who doesn't? At least this company acknowledges it and can put in place the necessary processes to make it happen. Then, the management team must make these processes excellent.

Our relationships with regulatory bodies must be such that we can influence/anticipate the rules of health care provisioning in our market.

Some very 'interesting' processes need to be excellent to accomplish this Critical Success Factor.

We must be more cost-effective than our competitors.

Simple, direct, and to the point, but what a difference it will make when they succeed.

Customers will acknowledge the superior quality and speed of our response to their needs.	From a petrochemical company.
We must accomplish a sustainable and profitable market share in the USA by financial year 1993–94.	From a Danish company.
We must achieve equality between customer requirements and what we deliver.	From a medical products company.
We must make it easier for customers to do business with us than with competitors.	From the same company. This simple expression of need would have a powerful impact on competitiveness, if accomplished.
We must expand our range of offerings to cater for the changing needs of our growing and ageing clientele.	From a company in the leisure and travel industry.
We must create the right working environment to attract, motivate, and retain highly skilled specialists.	From a scientific research and services group. Again, the word 'and' is acceptable here.
We must get rid of our high stools and quill pen image without impairing our reputation for security and stability.	From an insurance company.
We must establish the credibility of our North Sea exploration group in the eyes of corporate headquarters in the United States.	From an oil company. This is inwardly focused, but critically necessary in the eyes of the management team at the time.

We must avoid transfer of function to central government by demonstrating our competence and greater ability to provide and manage community services and facilities.	From a local authority in the United Kingdom, fighting against increasing control from central government.
We must anticipate the impact of technology changes on our products, in our target markets, faster than the competition.	From a petrochemical company.
We must bring our people along.	This was from the CEO of a multinational oil company. It was the last Critical Success Factor on the list. He looked at the preceding Factors and said, 'We can't do these unless we bring our people along'. So it was necessary. As a whole, the *entire* list was then regarded as sufficient.

These examples of Critical Success Factors are all fairly simple statements. Mostly, they describe the way things are *not* today. They are challenging requirements. Critical Success Factors tend to wake you up in the middle of the night in a cold sweat; that is how important they are. And because they are so broad in scope, they cannot be made the responsibility of *one* person; they are jointly owned by the entire top-management team.

But they *must* be accomplished. They are critical. *How* they are accomplished is by being rather better at the business processes the excellence of which is necessary for their success. Finding these most critical processes is the subject of the next chapter.

7
Finding the most critical business processes

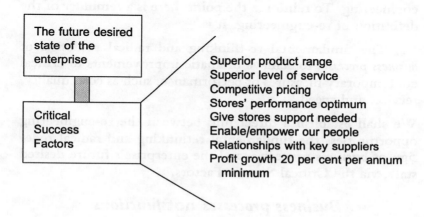

The future desired state of the enterprise	Superior product range
	Superior level of service
	Competitive pricing
	Stores' performance optimum
Critical Success Factors	Give stores support needed
	Enable/empower our people
	Relationships with key suppliers
	Profit growth 20 per cent per annum minimum

Figure 7.1 What Doppler Electronics had achieved midway through the first day of their study

Figure 7.1 shows where the Doppler Electronics Board had got to by lunchtime on the first day of their study:

- they know what they are *collectively* being paid for — to move their company forward to its future desired state
- they have agreed what they *collectively* have to do out-standingly well — the Critical Success Factors — to accomplish the future desired state of Doppler Electronics.

These are *shared* responsibilities. Critical Success Factors are not usually amenable to direct improvements — their scope is too broad. It is what will be *done* differently, in a number of different parts of the enterprise, that will ensure the achievement of each and every Critical Success Factor. The things that are done (or should be done) — the activities, if you prefer — are the business processes. It is the improved performance of individual business processes, and the effective exploitation of their mutual dependencies, that will achieve the Critical Success Factors. They will remain empty slogans unless the needed improvements in the processes are identified and implemented. This is at the heart of business re-engineering. To reinforce the point, here is a reminder of the definition of re-engineering. It is:

'... The fundamental re-thinking and radical re-design of *business processes* to achieve dramatic improvements in critical contemporary measures of performance, such as cost, quality, service, and speed.'

We shall establish a direct link between the re-engineering opportunities, the fundamental rethinking and radical redesign of business processes, and the enterprise's future desired state, via the Critical Success Factors.

Business processes not *functions*

In contrast with the Critical Success Factors, which can contain quite colourful language — remember 'We must have the finest marketing skills in Europe', for example — business process descriptions should be expressed in quite cool language. For example:

- 'Select suppliers'
- 'Bill customers'
- 'Develop new products'
- 'Process income tax returns'.

They look banal and familiar, especially after the excitement of looking to the future that was involved in creating the list of Critical Success Factors. Processes, though, usually have long lives, much longer than those of the Critical Success Factors. If you bill customers or develop new products, for example, you will probably want to continue performing these processes until the enterprise no longer exists. So, business processes deserve the investments needed to improve them to the level of competitive excellence. Then, perhaps, the enterprise will *continue* to exist, successfully.

Many of today's business processes will have been performed in the enterprise since the day it was created. And many of them will have been performed rather badly ever since.

The reason is simple. Few enterprises have even formally *identified* their business processes, let alone measured the quality with which they are performed. Most enterprises today are organized by function. Functional excellence is the basis for the reward system and each member of the top-management team tends to be the head of a function, such as Sales, Finance, Manufacturing, Surgery, Administration, Legal, Distribution, Personnel, and so on. But customers directly see or otherwise experience customer-visible *processes*, not functions. They also experience the consequences of the *invisible* processes, those internal to the enterprise that result in the products and services which will be compared with those of competitors.

For example, the 'Bill customers' process is a highly visible one. Notice that it is not the same as 'invoicing'. This may be the name of a department, usually within the Finance function, that produces the actual invoices. You can imagine walking down a corridor and seeing a label on a door, 'Invoicing Department'. Go in and you will find a manager and some well-trained, dedicated people working hard and using expensive technology to produce invoices, often to the total dissatisfaction of the customer. And it is not their fault.

The production of the invoice is one of the later stages of the process 'Bill customers'. This is a large, complicated, cross-functional process that presents many opportunities to get it wrong. It is easy to see why when we look at the different *functions* that may be involved in the process. For a manufacturing company, it might look like this.

Marketing	Keeping customer records up-to-date, and so on.
Sales	Negotiating the sale and creating the original purchase order.
Legal	Defining and modifying terms and conditions.
Distribution	Confirming which part of the order (or all of it) was delivered, when, where, and to whom.
Finance	Pricing, credit checks, invoicing, and so on.
Administration	Entering the purchase order. Providing the infrastructure to hold the whole thing together.
Service Engineering	Confirming that what was delivered was installed, and when.
Information Services	Providing the computer systems to maintain customer records, product files, price lists, the production of invoices, statements, and so forth.

Nowhere will you find a door with the label 'Bill customers' on it; the process is all over the place, and always has been. However, if you visit the head of each function, you will get a clear and convincing explanation of what a marvellous job each one of them is doing, and they are probably right, from a functional perspective. When you ask why the *process* may be less than excellent, you will be told that the fault lies in another function. Salespeople don't complete purchase orders properly, or they keep them in their brief cases. The people in the Legal Department won't make a decision about modified terms and conditions. Finance is ruminating for weeks over a claim for a credit. The computer systems for the different functions are incompatible and of varying antiquity. Some of them are constantly falling over. Program and database maintenance falls behind in the excitement of creating new systems. And so on.

If someone tries to sort out the *process*, they find themselves in the midst of boundary wars between the different functions, all of which may individually be very good.

From the customer's perspective, the process as a whole may be quite awful — invoices are late, sent to the wrong address, are incomplete, incomprehensible, they do not include credits that were agreed three months ago, and so on. The customer may spend three or four days a month trying to reconcile the billing problems, thereby adding unnecessary costs at their end, and finally refusing to pay until the seller gets it right. This is the lose–lose situation referred to earlier. And the bigger loser is probably the seller, because the customer in such a situation is likely to decide to put up with a (possibly) inferior price performance from the competition, just to get rid of the hassle of the seller's bad 'Bill customers' process.

(When I was a salesman, despite my best efforts, I found myself fighting a prolonged war with my employer on a customer's behalf for credits that had been negotiated and agreed a year earlier. The bad performance of the 'Bill customers' process really got in the way of the process that I was *supposed* to be engaged in, namely, 'Offer products for sale'. And I was not alone.)

The process 'Develop new products' is normally an invisible business process, though some companies have made it customer-visible by involving their customers in it, to the mutual benefit of both. Again, this is not the same as 'product development', another functional label.

Like 'Bill customers', the process 'Develop new products' is very cross-functional. If it is to create products that the market-place wants or needs, at competitive prices (which means at competitive total cost), it cannot be left solely to the people in the Product Development Department. For example, the people close to the market-place have to be involved in identifying and sizing the opportunity, defining the characteristics of the needed new product. Manufacturing have to be involved to ensure that what is developed is capable of being manufactured to the highest quality at a competitive cost. And so forth.

Question 3 requires the answers to be expressed in business process terms, not functions. Answering it usually involves a big challenge to the status quo, but it has to be done. Follow the thread back. The answers are merely a consequence of the agreed future desired state of the enterprise.

It is vital that the business processes are truly owned by the enterprise doing the study. Quite often I have found that a process on the list actually belongs in another part of the enterprise, often in corporate headquarters. If it belongs to someone else, you can't own it.

Executive process ownership — a necessary condition

Every critical process identified while answering Question 3 must have a unique owner. That owner must be a member of the management team that agreed the future desired state, identified the Critical Success Factors, and decided which business processes are essential for their achievement. This *individual* ownership of business processes is in contrast with the *shared* ownership of the future desired state and the Critical Success Factors.

Business processes are where improvements must happen, resources allocated, measurements made. Their performance is what distinguishes the winners from the losers. It is because their present and future performance is critical to the success of the enterprise that they need to be owned at the highest level in the enterprise. These processes normally have very strong dependencies on each other, too. This all requires individual ownership, yet a team approach. (All of the key dependencies will be revealed to the Doppler Electronics management team by the end of the second day of their study.)

Process ownership should not be delegated to someone lower

down in the owner's function. Ownership means responsibility and accountability for the present and future performance of the process. Only people at top management level can resolve the cross-functional issues involved in improving (or re-engineering) processes like 'Bill customers' or 'Develop new products' to competitive excellence. And it gets a lot easier to work as a team when these mutual dependencies have been flushed out.

The list of most critical processes — the result of answering Question 3 — will be short. Every member of the top-management team should own at least one of the most critical processes, but not more than two. Unlike the Critical Success Factors, business processes *can* be prioritized, so you should be able to allocate the finite, limited resources of the enterprise to those processes that are the most critical.

Some enterprises have instituted business process ownership, then allowed it to be delegated. What happens next is this. Consider the process 'Develop new products' again. Typically, the owner of this process would be the Director of the Research and Development Department. The Director then delegates 'management' of the process to someone in the Research and Development function. This person's job is to do all of the good 'quality' activities on behalf of the owner, who is above such things. A new job title is created: Manager of Development Quality. And this describes it exactly, because all of the improvements take place within the Research and Development *function*. The process 'manager' is too low down in the organization to have sufficient influence over what happens beyond the function's boundaries. The process itself, though, is truly cross-functional, as we have seen, and all the major improvement opportunities will be found *between* the various functions. So, we end up with small, local, triumphs of improvement within an already quite excellent function. The big opportunities remain unexploited. The result is that high cost, less than excellent products still emerge for a market-place that does not want them anyway.

67

This is not overdramatizing the situation. I have witnessed this sterile delegation of ownership many times. In the mid 1980s, for example, IBM Europe was engaged in implementing Total Quality Management. Key European-level processes were identified. The owners were the vice-presidents at the top of the European organization. One of the processes was concerned with billing. The owner was the Vice-President of Administration. A so-called 'Quality Council' was created to do the actual work, exactly in accordance with the Total Quality Management textbooks. But every member of it was from within the Administration function. Naturally, the really big opportunities were missed. (I understand that things have improved since then.)

Process re-engineering demands a holistic view across the enterprise and process ownership at the top. And that means an active, hands-on ownership, driven by an appropriate reward system.

Define processes clearly

It is essential to have a very clear definition of each business process. The language has to be precise and unambiguous, from the perspective of the management team concerned. This last point is important. The same words can legitimately mean quite different things to different teams. Indeed, it can be a way to differentiate one enterprise from another. For example, for Company A, the process 'Manufacture products' might include the activities of procurement of parts and raw materials as subprocesses. Its management team views them as subprocesses within the process 'Manufacture products'.

That is how it is in their business. To Company B, however, the process 'Manufacture products' might include only the activities of *making* the products. That is how it is in their business.

This means that each business process must have a clearly defined boundary. Without such a boundary, you do not know what is inside the process and what is outside it (see Figure 7.2).

68

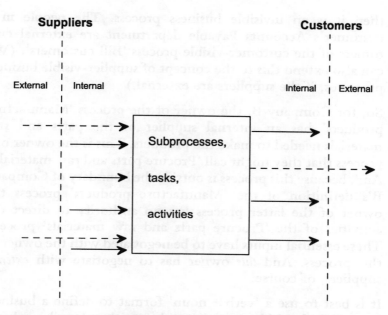

Figure 7.2 Establishing the boundaries of business processes

Inside the process are subprocesses, tasks, and activities, such as those needed to procure parts and raw materials in the case of Company A. Because these are an integral part of the process, they are all owned by the owner of the process. The owner is presumed to have the authority to direct what happens inside the process. So the Company A owner of the 'Manufacture products' process has the responsibility and authority to procure parts and raw materials needed for manufacturing the products.

Outside the process are its 'suppliers' and 'customers'. Suppliers are the providers of inputs to the process. Customers are the users of its outputs. Suppliers and customers may be internal to the enterprise or external, that is, beyond the boundary of the enterprise, or both. Clearly, if a business process has external customers, then it is a customer-visible process. If there are no external customers, then it is an invisible business process. The people in a customer's Accounts Payable department are external customers of the customer-visible process 'Bill customers'. (We can also extend this to the concept of supplier-visible business processes, if the suppliers are external.)

So, for Company B, the owner of the process 'Manufacture products' has an internal supplier of the parts and raw materials needed to make the products. This is the owner of a process that they might call 'Procure parts and raw materials'. And, because this process is outside the boundary of Company B's definition of the 'Manufacture products' process the owner of the latter process has no authority to direct the activities of the 'Procure parts and raw materials' process. These essential inputs have to be negotiated with the owner of this process. And *this* owner has to negotiate with *external* suppliers, of course.

It is best to use a 'verb + noun' format to define a business process. It should be an active verb, one that describes what is being *done*. Examples of such verbs are, educate, train, bill, develop, modify, select, forecast, manufacture, procure, advertise, negotiate. When we add the appropriate noun to the verb, we get an explicit description of the process:

- bill customers
- manufacture products
- educate and train personnel
- select and certify suppliers
- procure parts and raw materials
- merchandise products
- announce new products.

Some important points to note.

1 Just as in the wording of Critical Success Factors, avoid using 'and' in a definition of a process. The test for whether or not it can be used is simple: if the same *ownership* is appropriate for the parts that are coupled with 'and', it is all right to use it. So, 'Educate and train personnel' is probably acceptable

because, in most enterprises, the same owner would be responsible for both. The same might also apply to 'Select and certify suppliers'. However, this is up to the individual management team to decide — like everything else. A different team might take the view that certification of key suppliers should be owned by someone who is not involved in selecting them, for example.

2 The definition of a process must describe only the activity, *not* how well it should be performed. This means that adjectives and adverbs of quality should be excluded. Thus, 'Bill customers' is a process, but 'Bill customers accurately and on time' is a target. It describes how well the process should be performed. It might even be a description of the future desired state of the process (the subject of the next chapter) but it is not a process.

Many senior managers find this quite difficult, at first. They are accustomed to setting targets, so they tend to think in target terms. Examples which are often proposed as business processes include:

- reduce costs
- improve morale
- understand the local environment
- increase sales
- improve customer satisfaction
- generate demand
- develop good forecasts
- know the market requirements
- develop competitive new products.

These do all conform to the 'verb + noun' format, but they are *not* business processes. They all have one thing in common: they describe the desired result, not the activities necessary to achieve it. In fact, if we add the words 'We must' to each one of them, they could become candidates for a list of Critical Success Factors!

There is a simple rule that you can use to test whether or not you have created a real business process.

> **Write the process down.**
>
> **Read it.**
>
> **If what you read describes the *result* that you want, it is not a process.**

It would be splendid to reduce costs or improve morale, of course. But this *result* will follow only if improvements are made to the *processes* that add costs or influence morale.

3 The verb 'manage' should never appear in a definition of a process, nor similar verbs like 'administrate'. These also have the sense of describing a desired state, or result, such as 'Manage inventories'. But the main reason for banning such words is that they can lock you into today's way of thinking and doing things. Once you allow the word 'manage' to appear, it becomes difficult to avoid creating a business process list that looks like this:

- manage personnel
- manage customer relations
- manage product development
- manage procurement
- manage finance
- manage inventories
- manage administration
- manage sales
- manage marketing.

And we are back to functional descriptions again. These simply describe the way things are being done today. For example, the wine company, described earlier, had the problem of high interest rates and the Critical Success Factor 'We must dramatically reduce our inventory levels by ... (date)'. The management team might then decide that the process to achieve it would be called 'Manage inventories'. This, though, presumably, is what somebody has been trying to do for years, without great success in this case. No. It requires the excellent performance of a number of *real* business processes, in a number of different parts of the company, to achieve the (necessary) result of a dramatic reduction in inventories. This set of processes might include some or all of the following processes:

- Forecast product sales
- Market products
- Advertise products
- Offer products for sale
- Process customer orders
- Distribute products
- Monitor inventories
- Monitor supplier performance.

Bad performance of any one or all of these could be the reason for excessively high inventories. And most of them are beyond the power of whoever has had 'Manage inventories' as a job description. However, the result of improving them individually to competitive excellence, and supporting their mutual dependencies would bring about a dramatic reduction in inventories. (It would help the rest of the business, too!) So, it is the combined efforts of up to eight top-management owners of eight critical business processes that would bring about what is described in the definition of re-engineering, namely a '... radical re-design of business processes to achieve dramatic improvements in ... '. It is their combined efforts that will cushion the company against the effects of very high interest rates. This is *not* a result of improving the 'process' 'Manage inventories'.

'Sell' is another forbidden verb, for similar reasons. Consider the phrase 'Sell products'. It is tempting to list this as a business process, but it is actually the hoped-for result. It is the way that you 'Offer products for sale' that is compared with your competitors (*and* product price performance *and* other customer-visible processes, of course) and which can distinguish one seller from another, in the eyes of the customer.

This is not pedantry. If you allow imprecise or sloppy descriptions of your critical business processes now, you will

73

prejudice all the future analysis. And the purpose of the analysis is to reveal your best opportunities for improving Total Competitiveness/Effectiveness.

Table 7.1 includes a large number of descriptions of business processes collected from enterprises in a wide variety of industries. Only a few of them are industry-specific, however. Some may be near equivalents of others. Each one of them was considered to be critical for at least one management team. Use them as a menu for selecting the business processes that are most appropriate for your enterprise today. Change the words to suit your industry, of course. For example, 'Advertise products' might more appropriately be called 'Advertise financial management services', if this is your business.

The list is not meant to be exhaustive. You will probably need to create your own enterprise-specific descriptions of processes, but do follow the guidelines, given earlier but summarized below, when you write your descriptions of your business processes:

- verb + noun
- the *process*; not the desired result
- active, 'doing' verbs.

Table 7.1 A selection of business processes

Advertise products
Advise/draft/negotiate terms and conditions and contracts
Advise on alliances/alliance strategies
Announce new products
Answer customer enquiries
Bill customers
Collect debt
Communicate company policy and values
Define future skill needs
Define new product requirements

Define physical space requirements
Define/review customer service standards
Define/review product handling standards
Define security strategies
Deliver products
Demonstrate products
Design product packaging
Develop/review motivation plan
Develop review personnel development plans
Develop and maintain the fabric of the city
Distribute products
Document products for registration
Educate/train customers
Educate/train employees
Educate/train suppliers
Forecast cash flows
Forecast product volumes
Identify/cultivate relationships with key individuals
Identify/negotiate acquisitions
Identify target markets/customers
Inform management of legal developments
Invest liquid funds
Launch new products
Lobby government agencies
Lobby professional agencies
Maintain customer records
Maintain/service installed products
Manufacture products
Market products
Merchandize products
Monitor and report delivery performance
Monitor the competition
Monitor consumer trends
Monitor customer complaints
Monitor customer payments
Monitor customer's/prospect's business
Monitor customer satisfaction
Monitor emerging environmental issues

Monitor fashion trends
Monitor financial performance
Monitor inventories
Monitor legislation
Monitor key account activity
Monitor personnel motivation
Monitor the political environment
Monitor product performance
Monitor product quality
Monitor security of sensitive material
Monitor strategic alliance partner performance
Monitor supplier performance
Monitor technology opportunities
Monitor total costs
Negotiate budget
Negotiate customer requirements
Negotiate product supply
Offer products for sale
Pay suppliers
Plan facilities requirements
Plan product demand
Price products
Process customer orders
Process insurance claims
Promote the company
Purchase parts and raw materials
Recruit personnel
Release designs for manufacture
Research the market-place
Review/modify terms and conditions
Route shipments
Select and certify suppliers
Survey personnel satisfaction
Select sales and distribution channels
Track shipments
Track vehicle movements

The Critical Success Factor/business process matrix

Now we can rejoin the Board of Doppler Electronics, after lunch on the first day of their study. They are about to identify their most critical business processes, which will be their answer to Question 3.

The Doppler management team began by scanning a menu of business processes, like that given in Table 7.1. They used it to discuss and identify a number of business processes that they agreed were essential for the achievement of their Critical Success Factors. There were 14 of them, initially, which were:

- define market strategies
- develop new stores
- procure products
- order products for warehouses
- order products for stores
- deliver products to stores
- merchandize products
- monitor the competition
- refurbish existing stores
- monitor product quality
- monitor customer complaints
- establish human resource needs
- review technology opportunities
- review financial performance.

The Doppler management team knew exactly what each process meant to them, in their business.

It is not necessary for this list to be complete. The analysis that follows will ensure that *all* critical business processes for achieving the Critical Success Factors will be identified, and, thereby, following the thread back, achieving the future desired state for Doppler Electronics.

Each individual Critical Success Factor is different, but all are equally critical. Any one will only be achieved if certain business processes are excellent. Finding those processes, for each Critical Success Factor, is at the heart of this technique.

The Doppler team began with their first Critical Success Factor, 'Each consumer must perceive ours to be a superior product range', and considered their chosen list of 14 business processes. Then the question was asked, 'Which processes must be performed outstandingly well for us to be confident that we accomplish Critical Success Factor 1?'

The Doppler team decided that each of the following processes from their list would have a primary impact on achieving it.

- define market strategies
- procure products
- order products for warehouses
- order products for stores
- deliver products to stores
- merchandize products
- monitor the competition
- monitor product quality
- monitor customer complaints.

This means that each of the above processes *must exist and be excellent* to accomplish Critical Success Factor 1. That is, each of those processes is *necessary*. Now we test for sufficiency. The question to be answered is: 'Are these processes *sufficient* (if excellent) to accomplish Critical Success Factor 1?'

If the answer is 'Yes', we can move on to find the necessary and sufficient processes for Critical Success Factor 2. If the answer is 'No', we must identify the necessary *additional* process or processes needed to satisfy the sufficiency condition for accomplishing Critical Success Factor 1. That is why it is not necessary to start the analysis with a complete list of business processes. A rigorous test of sufficiency for each Critical Success Factor will flush out all of the missing critical business processes.

The Doppler team were not satisfied that the identified list of necessary processes for Critical Success Factor 1 *would* be sufficient. What was missing? Only they could answer this question. Eventually, they decided that the process 'Identify and cultivate relationships with key opinion formers' was necessary to ensure Critical Success Factor 1. For the Doppler team, the 'key opinion formers' included certain journalists and others in the media who wrote and spoke about consumer electronics products and their retail outlets. If this process was excellent, Doppler would always get good media coverage in terms of product range, service levels, store location, comfort, and so forth. Adding this process made the list *sufficient* for Critical Success Factor 1, in the opinion of the Doppler team — and there is no better qualified group of people on the planet to say so. Significantly, this critical process did not exist in Doppler Electronics at the time the study was made.

Now they could move on to Critical Success Factor 2, a totally different one needing excellence in a totally different set of business processes.

Figure 7.3 shows a convenient technique for asking the questions and displaying the answers. At the top, we have Doppler's future desired state — a constant reminder of what it is all about; the origin of the thread. Across the top are Doppler's eight Critical Success Factors. Down the left-hand side are their critical business processes, now enlarged in number from 14 to 18 as a result of applying the sufficiency test for processes per Critical Success Factor.

The 'X's entered on the matrix represent where an agreed answer of 'Yes' was given to the question, 'Which processes must be performed outstandingly well for us to be confident of achieving this Critical Success Factor?' So, under the first Factor, you will see an 'X' against all the processes listed earlier, *plus* the new process 'Identify and cultivate relationships with key opinion formers', which was added to satisfy the test of sufficiency.

Critical Success Factor 2 is completely different, but equally critical: 'We must convince consumers that we offer a superior level of service'. It requires excellence in a different set of business processes. Notice that three new additional

| Doppler Electronics' future desired state: 'We shall maximize the Total Competitiveness of Doppler Electronics' | | | | | | | | | | |

Business processes	Superior product range 1	Superior level of service 2	Competitive pricing 3	Stores perform optimally 4	Give stores the support they need 5	Enable/empower our people 6	Relationships with key suppliers 7	Profit growth 20% per year, minimum 8	Count	Quality
1 Define market strategies	X	X	X	X	X		X	X	7	C
2 Develop new stores		X			X	X	X	X	5	C
3 Procure products	X		X				X	X	4	D
4 Order products for warehouses	X			X	X		X		4	D
5 Order products for stores	X	X		X	X				4	D
6 Deliver products to stores	X	X		X	X				4	B
7 Merchandize products	X	X	X	X	X		X		6	C
8 Monitor the competition	X	X	X		X		X	X	6	C
9 Refurbish existing stores		X		X	X	X	X	X	6	B
10 Monitor product quality	X		X		X		X		4	D
11 Monitor customer complaints	X	X	X	X	X	X	X		7	D
12 Establish human resource requirements		X		X	X	X		X	5	C
13 Review technology opportunities		X		X	X	X	X	X	6	C
14 Review financial performance			X	X				X	3	B
15 Identify/cultivate key opinion formers	X	X	X		X		X		5	E
16 Define/review customer service standards		X		X	X	X			4	C
17 Monitor personnel motivation		X		X	X	X		X	5	E
18 Communicate company policy and values		X	X	X	X		X		5	C
19										
20										

Figure 7.3   Doppler's Critical Success Factor/Business Process Matrix

processes have appeared at the end of the list with 'X's by them for for Critical Success Factor 2. As before, these were added as a result of the sufficiency test. These are:

- define/review customer service standards
- monitor personnel motivation
- communicate company policy and values.

With this matrix completed, the management team of Doppler had an extremely valuable document, on just a single piece of A4 paper:

1 it shows their agreed future desired state

2 it shows their agreed Critical Success Factors

3 it shows *all* the most important business processes of their company for achieving its future desired state, via the Critical Success Factors that were agreed among them.

The matrix is not only valuable for what it contains; it is also valuable for what it reveals. Consider processes 1 and 11, 'Define market strategies' and 'Monitor customer complaints', respectively. Each of them has a primary impact on the accomplishment of seven Critical Success Factors. Therefore, any underperformance of these two processes will have a dramatic impact on Doppler's future desired state. If both of them are already excellent, then fine. The management team should be concerned with *maintaining* their competitive excellence. On the other hand, if they are not excellent now, then they had better be improved to excellence as soon as possible. Here lies the basis for prioritizing the critical business processes.

The most critical business processes

Now, the Doppler team could move on to prioritizing their business processes, to find their most critical business processes.

There are two elements that combine to determine the ranking of processes on the matrix. These are the number of

Critical Success Factors that are impacted by each process, and the quality of each process today. The first is easy to determine — just count the number of 'X's in each horizontal row. Thus, 'Define market strategies' has a primary impact on seven Critical Success Factors, while 'Order products for warehouses' has a primary impact on four.

For process quality, the Doppler management team used a subjective scale as follows:

A = Excellent   C = Fair   E = The process does not
B = Good   D = Bad   effectively exist today

Such a scale lacks *mathematical* rigour, but it is good enough for our purpose. This is not an exact science. The Doppler team are simply being asked to judge — even roughly — how well they believe they are performing their critical business processes, so they should be able to tell the difference between them, even with a rough scale like this. Moreover, they are being asked to judge the process quality now, knowing the future desired state for Doppler Electronics, and knowing what their Critical Success Factors are. In other words, perceiving how good the processes were yesterday is not good enough. The quality of the business processes must be judged in the light of the new criteria agreed before lunch.

Not surprisingly, under these conditions, very few management teams agree that *any* of their processes are excellent. Almost always, they discover processes that are critical, but which they have to award an E (the process does not effectively exist today). The reason for this is that the processes in place today in most enterprises are those that were needed last year, or 5 years ago or 50. The fresh challenge to the status quo in searching for the Critical Success Factors therefore almost invariably reveals processes that *should* exist from now on, but do not exist today. Not surprisingly, the brewing company described earlier with the Critical Success Factor 'We must acquire retailing skills' had a number of critical processes on their matrix that were to do with retailing and which were given an E. Their existing processes, most of them over 200 years old, were restricted to the processes of brewing, beer distribution, and pub management. They were all that had been needed. And they were pretty good.

A large shipping company in Israel discovered that one of its most critical processes was in the area of managing political influence. The old-established processes of the business were reasonably well performed, but the fulcrum of success (as they saw it), their major competitive opportunity, lay in the lobbying process. Top-level ownership quickly followed. Political lobbying had been done in the past, but it was fragmentary, informal and peripheral to the company's normal business activities. Subsequently, though, it was resourced and managed as a most critical process.

Usually by this stage, there is no difficulty in getting agreement on the quality of the processes. For a list of 18 processes, such as that produced by the Doppler team, I find it takes only about an hour. Sometimes there is some disagreement. A process, such as 'Establish human resource needs', may be declared to be good in one part of the enterprise, but bad in another, for example. To get around this, score the process as B/D. Then delete the B. We are taking a holistic view of the enterprise. Excellence is the only acceptable standard for its critical business processes. If it is agreed to be merely 'good in parts', but bad elsewhere, it is bad until the *whole* thing is good. And then, the whole thing has to be improved until it is *excellent*.

Figure 7.3 shows Doppler's completed matrix, including the count of impacts on Critical Success Factors for each business process and the management team's agreement as to the quality with which the process is performed (they are in the two right-hand columns).

Now we have all the raw materials to rank Doppler's critical business processes. The information contained in the two right-hand columns of their matrix is simply transferred to the grid shown in Figure 7.4.

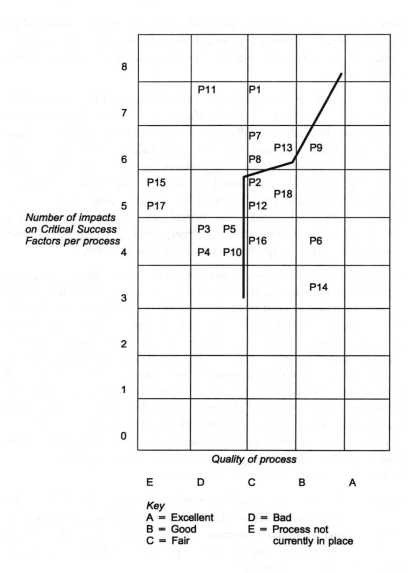

Figure 7.4 Finding the most critical business processes for Doppler Electronics

The vertical axis gives the number of impacts on the Critical Success Factors of each business process. With eight Critical Success Factors, the possible range is from zero to eight. The horizontal axis gives the quality rating of each business process, on the scale A to E. The processes on this grid are positioned according to their combined Critical Success Factor count and quality, as follows.

Process 11, 'Monitor customer complaints', has a primary impact on seven Critical Success Factors and its quality is D, bad. We can call it a 7-D process, and position it in the seventh square up, second along from the left. It is identified there as 'P11' (Process 11). Similarly, Process 14, 'Review financial performance', is a 3-B process. It impacts three Critical Success Factors and its quality is B, good. It is identified as P14 in the 3-B square, third from the bottom and second from the right. And so on.

Now we can prioritize.

The most critical processes are those tending to the top-left corner of the grid. They have the highest numeric impact on the Critical Success Factors and they have the worst quality ratings.

It can be helpful when ranking to assign a numerical value to the quality factors, thus:

- A = 1
- B = 2
- C = 3
- D = 4
- E = 5

Each square on the grid can now be given a number corresponding to the result of multiplying its Critical Success Factor count and its quality. So, the uppermost left-hand square will have the highest score ($8 \times 5 = 40$), the square to its right will have the score ($8 \times 4 = 32$) and that below the top left square ($7 \times 5 = 35$), and so on.

The Doppler team decided to concentrate on those processes with a score of 16 or more, that is, those to the left of the line shown in Figure 7.4. From the Doppler team's point of view, these 11 processes were the most critical, at that time. Another management team might have decided to focus only on a smaller number of processes or even only one of them to start with. Yet another team, on all 18 of them. It is a matter of judgement, and the best-qualified people to make it are the top management team. The number 11 was also a convenient number for the Doppler Board, which comprised 8 people, so 3 members owned 2 processes, while the rest owned 1 each.

It was now early evening on the first day of their study. Doppler's agreed list of most critical processes was as follows:

- define market strategies
- procure products
- order products for warehouses
- order products for stores
- merchandize products
- monitor the competition
- monitor product quality
- monitor customer complaints
- review technology opportunities
- identify/cultivate relationships with key opinion formers
- monitor personnel motivation.

The management team was now equipped with:

1 a clear understanding of each most critical process

2 an agreed understanding of the current level of quality of performance for each of those processes, which was decided during the creation of Doppler's Critical Success Factor/ business process matrix; it defines the starting point for improvement.

Now they are ready to apply themselves to Question 4, 'What is the future desired state of each critical process?'

Before moving on to this, here are a few pointers to help you produce your own enterprise-specific matrix, and then find your most critical processes using this technique.

1 It is useful to work with a blank matrix on a transparency and use an overhead projector. This enables everyone to see what is happening simultaneously and to focus on the particular issue being addressed.

2 The positioning of each 'X' on the matrix is important. Their number for any process is a key ingredient in ranking the processes. (The recommended approach to the other element, quality of performance of a process, has already been discussed. If the process is bad in parts, work with the quality of the *worst* part.)

Each 'X' means that the business process concerned will have a *primary* impact on the achievement of the particular Critical Success Factor under consideration, but it is very tempting to put an 'X' almost everywhere, at first. Here is a way round this problem if it occurs.

Many people are more comfortable about deciding whether the impact of a process on a Critical Success Factor is high, medium or low, so, instead of an 'X', enter 'H', 'M' or 'L' in each square — but use a *waterproof* pen for the 'H's, a *water-soluble* pen for the 'M's and 'L's. Then, when the last one has been considered, a quick wipe with a damp cloth will reveal only the 'H's, corresponding to a primary impact on the Critical Success Factors concerned. This is not a trick. It is just a way to make it easier to decide which are the primary impacts.

3 What about the critical processes that are on Doppler's Critical Success Factor/process matrix, but which are not in their list of most critical processes? There are seven of them:

- develop new stores
- deliver products to stores
- refurbish existing stores

- establish human resource needs
- review financial performance
- define/review customer service standards.

It does not mean that these processes are to be ignored. Indeed, in addition to these, there are other essential processes that do not even appear on the matrix — 'Pay employees', and 'Pay suppliers', for example. It is just that they are not on today's critical path. The Doppler team has merely decided which of their critical processes *are most in need of improvement*. These most critical processes represent a threat or an opportunity, depending on your point of view. *All* of the processes on their matrix have a primary impact on one or more of their Critical Success Factors, as we have seen. So, they should all be made competitively excellent. Just as important, they should not be allowed to deteriorate.

Doppler's approach to this was to give ownership also of the less critical processes to individual Board members. The owners were responsible for monitoring them to ensure that their performance did not deteriorate. There was enough work to do, in their view, in improving the most critical processes — all 11 of them. Later, the owners could turn their attention to the less critical ones, and improve *these* to competitive excellence.

4 Be prepared for surprises to appear in the agreed list of most critical processes. In most cases, a process will feature that does not even *exist* in the enterprise today. Yet it *has* to exist. This was the case with Doppler's 'Identify/cultivate relationships with key opinion formers', 'Monitor personnel motivation' and 'Communicate company policy and values'.

Frequently, people are surprised that something apparently mundane appears as a most critical business process, and thus has executive ownership. But the enterprise *demands* such a level of ownership. Follow the thread back: everything flows from the enterprise's future desired state. 'Monitor customer complaints' comes up frequently, as it did for Doppler Electronics. It is a natural consequence of today's environment of very good, very clever competitors, and a much more educated and demanding buyer population. (And you will find that 'Monitor customer complaints' is a key internal *supplier* of information to other critical business processes.)

Twenty years ago it might have been considered all right to give the task to a management trainee, to answer the telephone, and, '... say something soothing to them. But keep them off my back!' Today, a well-performed 'Monitor customer complaints' process can provide many opportunities to reduce costs, improve products and services, and *increase* customer satisfaction.

General Electric shows how this can be done.

A very senior manager owns the 'Monitor customer complaints' process in General Electric, and large investments have been made to ensure that it is done excellently. Anyone in the United States can call General Electric at Louisville, Kentucky, on a toll free '800' telephone number. General Electric spends about $8 million on the telephone calls alone, yet it makes a profit from this process.

The calls are taken by *very* well-trained General Electric personnel. This is not a job for a backpacker passing through town on a world tour and needing two or three weeks' work. The calls are handled sensitively. Studies in the United Kingdom and in the United States have shown that, if a customer's complaint is handled quickly and sensitively, customer loyalty is increased, and the customer buys from you again the next time. This is one way in which the process contributes to General Electric's profit; increased sales through increased customer loyalty.

Another direct contributor to profits is reduced warranty costs. Not only are the people taking the calls very well-trained, they have excellent information services support at their fingertips, including a database that contains the answers to more than half a million potential customer problems. Often, instead of sending an expensive service engineer, the problem can be easily fixed by the customer under the guidance of the person in Louisville. It could be as simple as, 'Try pushing the little red button at the back. It's the overload switch.' Result? An immediate fix to the customer's problem, a satisfied customer, using the appliance again, and a substantial avoidance of cost for General Electric. (However, one man telephoned and asked for guidance on how he could convert his black-and-white television set to colour, which might have taken a bit longer to achieve!)

Only about 10 per cent of calls are complaints. Something over 700 000 calls each year are from people wanting product information. This represents 700 000 new sales opportunities, per year, each one initiated by a real or prospective customer and handled by a trained General Electric employee. The investment in this process extends to General Electric dealers and agents, the people who own the process 'Offer products for sale'. (As in the case of Mars Confectionery, consumers do not normally buy products directly from General Electric.) The personnel in Louisville are on-line to over 2000 General Electric dealers and agents, who can immediately follow up, at a local level, any sales lead resulting from a call to Louisville.

It does not end there. The people taking the calls are also on-line to other business processes inside General Electric, for example, those concerned with manufacturing, procurement, design of maintenance schedules, the writing of instruction booklets, and so forth. This means that General Electric can react quickly to a product problem identified in the real world of consumers. Previously, General Electric was insulated from the people actually buying and using its products (and those of its competitors) by its dealers and agents. General Electric could only find out what the consumers' perceptions were of its products (and those of its competitors) by means of expensive market surveys, perhaps every two years or so. This process might be called 'Monitor customer satisfaction', a totally different process to 'Monitor customer complaints'. Do *this* well, and you can learn a lot from the process every single day. By the time the 'Monitor customer satisfaction' data is collected and analysed, it is too late: product cycle times are too short nowadays for such a coarse timeframe (the Japanese have reduced the time it takes to get a new consumer electronics product to about 180 days, from the moment the opportunity is identified to when the product is out there, earning revenue).

Like Mercedes, General Electric 'is in the right business', so it *had* to become more responsive to its market–place.

In the public sector, the Government of the UK is being driven by a combination of rising costs and pressure from the electorate to do something about the complaints procedure for the National Health Service. Payouts for medical malpractice went up from £60 million in 1990–91 to over £90 million in 1992–93. One idea is to establish a single, independent body to collect *all* National Health Service complaints and help patients who simply cannot come to terms with the mind-boggling bureaucracy. This would effectively mean that the process 'Monitor customer complaints' would be owned and operated outside of the enterprise. We shall see more examples analogous to this.

Another reason for apparently mundane-looking processes appearing on a list of most critical processes is changes in business methods. The process 'Select suppliers' was an activity done by people in the Buying Department 10 or 20 years ago. It still is, in many enterprises. And often, there is a large number of different suppliers.

Today, manufacturing companies and supermarkets are insisting on Just-In-Time delivery of products and other supplies. This keeps their costs down, but demands products of the highest quality from the suppliers. Close attention must be paid to the 'supplier-visible' business processes. Occasionally, a single supplier is involved, rather than a multitude. The potential impact on the business is now such that executive ownership of the process 'Select suppliers' becomes imperative.

So, expect surprises, and be glad that you found them.

Competitive adaptability

Notice that the processes placed on the grid used for ranking them (see Figure 7.4) can move either horizontally or vertically.

Horizontal movement to the right — in the direction of competitive excellence — will only come about if improvements are driven by the executive owners of the processes. Business processes do not spontaneously improve to become excellent. Rather, if you leave them alone, they deteriorate, which means that they move to the left.

Vertical movement of a process on the grid can only result from a re-evaluation of the impact of that process on all the Critical Success Factors, or a change in the Critical Success Factors themselves. After a year or so, the Doppler team should re-visit their future desired state. It may remain the same, but small (or even large) changes may be agreed with regard to a number of Critical Success Factors. This will require a re-evaluation of the impacts of business processes on them. These changes will then be reflected in the grid of Figure 7.4. But, after a year of sustained management attention to the most critical processes, their quality will be much higher — they will have moved towards the right of the grid. With the increase in the quality of performance of the critical processes, the business has become more adaptive to change, because it is much easier to respond to change when processes are already good than when they are bad.

If Doppler's management team had the luxury of there being no changes in their Critical Success Factors (and enough time) we can imagine them improving *all* of their most critical processes so that they moved to the right-hand side of the grid, that is, all of them would have been improved until they were excellent. *Then*, imagine a dramatic change — a new CEO, new, powerful competitors, new technology, changed consumer tastes, new legislation or whatever. The management team may then create a different future desired state, new or altered Critical Success Factors, but, when they create a new Critical Success Factor/process matrix, all their existing core processes will be A, excellent! Some additional processes will doubtless appear, some of which may be new to the business. But the management team is by now already rather good at improving its processes, putting new processes in place, and managing them so that they become excellent. Competitive excellence in the key business processes facilitates a very good state of adaptability to change. The management team would need only to focus on the *new* arrivals on their critical process list. And the next time there is a need to change, they will be even more adaptive.

Of course, they do *not* have this luxury of a static business environment, and sufficient time to improve their processes until they are excellent. Nobody has. This was *reductio ad absurdum* necessary to make the point. But, as long as they set off on the journey towards the competitive excellence of their key business processes, and they continue the journey, they will still be in a better state to respond to the next planned or unpredictable change than they would otherwise be.

The ability to react quickly to unpredictable change is a measure of the enterprise's ability to survive. Poor-quality business processes can be an Achilles' heel. So, the *journey* towards competitive excellence of key processes is worth while, even though you will never reach nirvana.

But the management team of Doppler Electronics cannot even *start* the journey yet. This is addressed in Question 4, 'What is the future desired state of each critical process?'

8

The future desired state of the most critical business processes

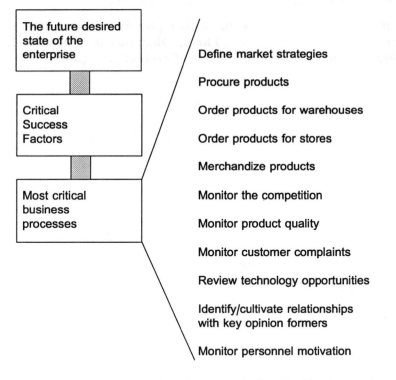

The future desired
state of the
enterprise

Critical
Success
Factors

Most critical
business
processes

Define market strategies

Procure products

Order products for warehouses

Order products for stores

Merchandize products

Monitor the competition

Monitor product quality

Monitor customer complaints

Review technology opportunities

Identify/cultivate relationships
with key opinion formers

Monitor personnel motivation

Figure 8.1   The stage Doppler Electronics had reached by the evening of
the first day of their study

Figure 8.1 shows where the Board of Doppler Electronics had got to by the evening of the first day of their study. Now they know which business processes have the biggest impact on the achievement of Doppler's future desired state; they know the things that have to be *done*. By the time they have their coffee break next morning, they will have agreed on how *well* those processes have to be done.

They had already agreed the current quality of these processes. None could be awarded an A (excellent), in their view. But excellence is the *only* acceptable quality, otherwise achieving the future desired state for Doppler Electronics will be unlikely. This state of *process* excellence is what is meant by the future desired state of each most critical process. Knowing the current quality and having a clear description of excellence defines the 'delta'; the gap that has to be closed between where the process is *now* and where it *needs* to be.

But what exactly does 'excellence' mean for a business process? Lowest cost? Highest *external* customer satisfaction? Highest *internal* customer satisfaction? Fastest performance? Most adaptive to changes? Most environmentally friendly? Something else? Some of these desirable targets may be in mutual conflict.

Back to the enterprise's future desired state

We must go back to the future desired state of the enterprise to resolve this.

> **Excellence of a business process is a description of its performance when it is making the maximum possible contribution to the enterprise's future desired state.**

Trade-offs and compromises will have to be made, of course, but the focus has to be on the agreed future desired state of the enterprise. This is a *strategic* focus, so tactical considerations should not be allowed to blur it. So, if a *process* future desired state is defined in a way that requires it to be the most environmentally friendly, for example, that focus must remain sharp, or it will never achieve this state. There is no point in adding, in six months' time, ' . . . and at a lower cost than our competitors'. You have to decide — using the enterprise's future desired state as the yardstick — then stay with it.

Notice that it is important *not* to use just one Critical Success Factor as a basis for defining a process future desired state. Critical Success Factors are often in mutual conflict; they cannot be prioritized. A process future desired state focused on just one of them could imply prioritization. *Each* and *all* of the Critical Success Factors must be accomplished. They are tightly coupled by the thread mentioned earlier to the enterprise's future desired state. The main work of the Critical Success Factors, which is to identify the competitive opportunities, is done now. They were agreed in order to discover the most critical processes. Do not set them aside, however. The top management team should be reminded of them constantly, to ensure that they do not forget what their *collective* responsibility is towards achieving the future desired state.

The need for top management to focus on the *quality* of the processes is illustrated by the approach of Robert Galvin when he was CEO of Motorola. Apparently he insisted that quality reports came first on the agenda of his top management meetings. Then he left before the financial results were discussed.

Consider the Komatsu mission, quoted earlier: 'We will encircle Caterpillar'.

To the best of my knowledge, the board of Komatsu did not use the technique described here, but we can imagine a list of Critical Success Factors being prepared as a result of arriving at this mission statement, which would lead to a list of most critical processes being made. Then, this very clear, enterprise–wide future desired state should make it relatively easy to define the state of competitive excellence required for each most critical process, that is, the future desired state of each process.

Remember, too, Midland Bank's mission: 'To become Britain's most recommended bank by 1995'.

This should provide some *very* clearly defined future desired states of processes.

We are back to how extremely important is the definition of the enterprise's future desired state. Ambiguity there leads to ambiguity in all that follows, including deciding the future desired states of the processes. These descriptions of the future desired states of the processes are the source of major re-engineering and other competitiveness projects.

Consider the two contrasting examples given earlier that might come from a region of the UK's National Health Service:

- 'The mortality rate in this region will improve at a faster year-on-year rate than the average for the UK'
- 'The general health of the population in this region will improve on a year-on-year basis at a faster rate than the average for the United Kingdom'.

It is obvious that important differences in the future desired states of the most critical business processes would result, depending on which future desired state for the *enterprise* is chosen.

In the same way, the democratically elected Prime Minister's 'We get re-elected' has a different set of processes (and future desired states of these processes) to the dictator's 'We stay in power'.

It does get more difficult when the enterprise's future desired state contains contrasting elements, such as the one quoted earlier:

'By end 1996, we will:

- hold relative market share versus Woodhouses and C. J. Barton

97

- be perceived by consumers as being the best place to shop for ladies' fashion items
- financially outperform Woodhouses and C. J. Barton.'

Nevertheless, though it is more difficult, the members of the top management team are the only people qualified to make the decision. In this case, it may be between financial performance and the perceptions of consumers. One way to resolve this is to fall back on the definition of Total Competitiveness/Effectiveness and use this as the basis for defining the future desired state of the processes.

'Total Competitiveness' is the result of multiplying:

1 relative product price performance and
2 relative customer satisfaction with all "customer-visible" business processes.'

'Relative' here means relative to the competition.

The process future desired state, then, is when it would be making the biggest possible contribution to Total Competitiveness/Effectiveness.

This was the approach taken by the Doppler Electronics team. For them, it was the obvious thing to do, given the generic nature of the enterprise's future desired state: 'We shall maximize the Total Competitiveness of Doppler Electronics'.

The first day's work ended at about 6 pm, after the Doppler team had agreed their most critical processes. They were given some guidelines for thinking about what a business process future desired state should be like, and a number of examples to stimulate the imagination (like those in Table 8.1, at the end of this chapter), but there was no formal work until the session started again at 8.30 am on the second (and last) day.

As the members of the team had time to reflect during the evening of the first day, the future desired states for each of the most critical process were agreed quite quickly. In effect, the management team had moved from something large, difficult, and shared — the future desired state of the enterprise — to a set of 11 future desired states of processes that were individually owned yet small enough to define projects to accomplish them — the basis for re-engineering the processes. The Doppler team's view of competitive excellence for their 11 most critical processes was as follows.

Doppler's process future desired states

Define market strategies

We have such a sufficiently clear knowledge about customers, consumers, competitors, consumer electronics products, and the market-place that we can always develop strategies to exploit our strengths to the total satisfaction of our customers.

The quality of this process was C, fair, and it had a primary impact on seven Critical Success Factors. The future desired state tells us why it was only fair at the time of the study. The management team's view was that their knowledge of customers, consumers, competitors, consumer electronic products, and the market-place was *not* sufficiently clear. This resulted in them developing strategies that did *not* exploit Doppler's strengths, and the customers were *not* always satisfied. Another management team might have found that they had clear enough information, but lacked the skills to translate it into good strategies. This would lead to a different future desired state for this same business process, of course. *Vive la différence!*

Procure products

Our relationship with suppliers is such that we always get fully competitive prices and priority supply of excellent quality products.

This is an invisible business process. Done badly, or even only to a fair standard, the result is higher costs than needed with a roll-on impact on pricing flexibility. It also has a deleterious impact on such customer-visible processes as 'Merchandize products', which depend upon the outputs of the 'Procure products' process.

The quality of the 'procure products' process was C, fair. Doppler's future desired state tells us that the relationship with suppliers was not as good as it should be. The result was that Doppler was paying more than it needed and/or it did not get priority supplies of products. Maybe their competitors did, however.

Order product for warehouses

Products are ordered for our warehouses to enable them to meet store orders and in a manner that matches the best cost standards in the industry.

The current quality was D, bad. This definition of the future desired state indicates that the service to the stores is not good enough and the costs are not competitive. Here, the focus for improvement is simultaneously on the level of service to the company's retail outlets *and* the internal efficiency of the operation.

Order products for stores

We know so much about our customers that we always have cost-effective availability of products.

If this is read in a negative manner, it describes the process as it was at the time of the study; D, bad: 'We do not know enough about our customers. In consequence, we sometimes have the wrong products in the wrong places at the wrong times or too many of them or not enough. And we sometimes pay too much for them.'

American Express illustrates the importance of knowing about your customers. It keeps details of over 450 attributes of its cardholders. This enables the process 'Offer products for sale' to be very effective because it is then possible to target very precisely the marketing of top-of-the-range goods as diverse as luggage, jewellery, cameras, consumer electronics (Doppler's business), fur coats, and so forth.

Merchandize products

Merchandizing will result from store-specific plans, reflecting the particular geographic, cultural, and social characteristics of each store, and will be developed in line with real-time knowledge of actual store-specific needs.

The quality was C, fair, and it had a primary impact on six Critical Success Factors. Doppler's future desired state for this process suggests that merchandizing had not been sufficiently discriminating between stores — leading to lost opportunities, and higher costs.

Monitor the competition

On a day-by-day basis, we are fully aware of the strengths and weaknesses of all our competitors, their current position in the market, and their strategies for the future.

This was another process that scored C, fair, with a primary impact on six Critical Success Factors. It tells us that Doppler has been taken by surprise in the past, and it hurt.

Monitor product quality

Every employee knows so much about the products we offer for sale that no customer can ever leave one of our stores with a defective product.

This process scored D, bad. There is therefore a large gap to close between the present state and the process future desired state, with equally large requirements to be placed on other processes of the company, 'Procure products', for example, and the processes of recruitment and employee education and training.

> **Monitor customer complaints**
>
> **We make it easy for customers to communicate with us. All complaints are handled to the customer's total satisfaction. Complaints are transmitted to the most appropriate manager so that action can be taken to prevent it being repeated. Customers acknowledge the superior speed and effectiveness of our response.**

This process was very high in the priority ranking. Its present quality was deemed D, bad, and it impacted seven Critical Success Factors, so it had to have an aggressively framed future desired state. The experience of General Electric, described earlier, shows how it can be done, with top management ownership and an appropriate level of investment.

> **Review technology opportunities**
>
> **We know about all technology opportunities appropriate to our business and we are ready to exploit effectively those that we chose, before our main competitors do.**

Creating this future desired state produced some revealing discussion among the Doppler team. The Chief Executive gave ownership of the process to his Director of Information Services. While the future desired state was being debated, the CEO suddenly asked me, 'Is this only related to information technology, or does it embrace other technologies? I've been assuming it's IT, which is why I gave it to Elizabeth, but we need to know about *all* technologies appropriate to our business! Do you want to take the broader brief, Liz?' She now monitors *all* technologies relevant to the retailing business — actively and thoroughly.

> **Identify/cultivate relationships with key opinion formers**
>
> **We are always bracketed with our two major competitors [named] as a leading retailer of consumer electronics products in all the media's comments.**

102

This process was in the E, process does not currently exist, category, and it had a primary impact on four Critical Success Factors. So, someone had to own it, put it in place and ensure that it operated to the standards of the process future desired state. The Chief Executive took ownership of this process.

Monitor personnel motivation

We know what our employees feel about those aspects of our business that influence their motivation, and its impact on productivity, in time and in sufficient detail for us to respond appropriately.

This was another E and it had a primary impact on five Critical Success Factors. Its future desired state reveals concerns that motivation problems may have been having an adverse effect on productivity and performance.

In Table 8.1, which follows, there is a selection of business processes, with descriptions of their future desired states. (To avoid repetition, Doppler's are not included in the Table). These examples are drawn from a wide spectrum of industries in a number of European countries. They are quite simple, straightforward statements. Again, our visitor from outer space might read them and exclaim 'Are things not *normally* like this here?'. But I have never come across any enterprise whose critical business processes are as good as these. Imagine the impact on competitiveness if they *were* to be this good.

The examples are provided to help you create your own descriptions of the future desired state of your business processes. You may be able to pick up some of them exactly as they are. Others will need modifying. Almost certainly, you will have to create entirely new ones for processes that are not represented in this limited sample.

Important: Notice that none of these descriptions mentions the *means* of accomplishing the future desired state of the process concerned, for exactly the same reason that the means should

103

not be included or implied in the *enterprise's* future desired state. Bear this in mind when creating your own process future desired states — just describe the state of competitive excellence, not the means of achieving it. This comes later, when we can define the re-engineering and other improvement projects. And don't set easy targets. Try to imagine a quantum change in process performance, something that will really differentiate this process from your competitors'. Think crazy. Imagine the impossible.

Table 8.1. A selection of business processes with descriptions of their future desired states

---

Announce new products

Announcement material is available, immediately there is an announcement, in every country where we market the products. It will be in the appropriate language and will be sensitive in text and illustrations to the national culture, and so on. Prices, terms and conditions, and any prerequisites will be clearly defined at the time of announcement.

Bill customers

All invoices are complete, accurate, on time, and sent to the right person at the right address. Find out what 'understandable' means to the customer, then do it.

Define future skill needs

There is a sufficiently clear and complete description of future skill needs that we can effectively plan recruitment and/or personnel education and training to meet the requirements at all times.

Define new product requirements

All specifications of new products will meet the needs, or anticipated needs, of known target customers, better than do those of our competitors.

Develop new products

New designs will be superior to those offered by the competition and will be capable of being manufactured at competitive cost.

Distribute products

All deliveries are complete and with zero defects on arrival. Deliveries are to the right address on the right date. The 'right date' means in accordance with the customer's needs *and* the customer is ready to accept delivery — all prerequisites are in place, such as training, cables, power and water supplies, buildings, and so on.

Distribute products

Products arrive complete, on time, to the user as required by the customer. (This is from a medical products company. The user is the surgeon; the customer is the hospital.)

Educate and train personnel

An effective education and training programme exists for all personnel. We secure their commitment to follow it and monitor its effectiveness via job performance and employee satisfaction surveys.

Identify target markets/customers

We have a sufficiently clear understanding of all market opportunities for our products that we can select the best potential winners for our products.

Lobby government and professional agencies

There are no nasty surprises in terms of regulations, laws, and so on. This means, if they are nasty but unavoidable, we know about them in time to respond or react effectively. Also, for professional bodies, we lobby effectively for laws and regulations that are compatible with our requirements.

Manufacture products

Products with zero defects are available for distribution to our customers in accordance with our requirements and at a competitive manufactured cost.

Market products

Products are offered for sale to customers and prospects who are aware of them — their benefits, prices, techniques, and so on — and they are ready to buy at an appropriate price/value relationship.

Monitor customer satisfaction

We have an accurate knowledge of the level of customer satisfaction, relative to the competition, for all our products *and* for all aspects of our business that are visible to our customers.

Monitor legislation

We know about all laws, regulations, codes of practice, customs, and so on, that are relevant to our business wherever we operate, to the extent that we are never taken by surprise.

Monitor the performance of strategic alliance partner(s)

We know how well each partner is performing against our agreed objectives, and they ag: :e.

Negotiate bio-safety testing (for a health-care company)

We always provide adequate, accurate biological testing results to our customers and regulatory agencies when they are required.

Negotiate commercial agreements

All are completed in order not to delay any project and are negotiated to a win–win position.

Negotiate product supply

All products are available for us to ship to customers in accordance with our requirements — timeliness, quality, quantity, safety tested, and so on. (This company was in the health care business in Europe. All of its products were imported from the parent company in the United States, hence the particular wording of this process future desired state.)

Negotiate selling channels/agencies

We have a clear understanding of the costs and benefits of alternative sales and distribution channels and we successfully negotiate the appointment of those we choose.

Process customer orders

The status of each customer's order is known to all who have a need to know from the moment the order is placed until billing is completed.

Promote the company

Our target audiences — customers, employees, shareholders, vendors, the media, governments, and the financial institutions — receive a clear and favourable understanding of the image we wish to create.

Promote the company (For a European division of a US-based multinational)

The corporate Board decision makers understand and acknowledge the benefits of participation in our industry and commit to the future of the business.

Review effectiveness of the sales network's reward and recognition system

We have a measurement system that enables us to understand and report on the effectiveness of our sales network's reward and recognition system to attract and retain a best-of-breed sales force.

Select and certify vendors

We successfully negotiate terms and conditions with those vendors we need to provide critical inputs to our company, to the disadvantage of our competitors.

9

The essential inputs for each process

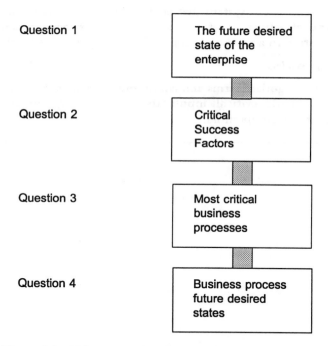

Question 1   The future desired state of the enterprise

Question 2   Critical Success Factors

Question 3   Most critical business processes

Question 4   Business process future desired states

Figure 9.1   Where Doppler Electronics are by coffee break on the second day of their study

The Board of Doppler Electronics has arrived at the point shown in Figure 9.1 by the time of the morning coffee break on the second day of their study.

Now they know what each individual member of the top management team has to do — to improve each most critical business process to a state of competitive excellence. But, knowing *how* to do this is a different matter.

Improvements relate partly to the internals of the process — the way subprocesses and activities are performed and resources are allocated. However, a major cause of a process being less than excellent is the poor quality or inadequate supply of inputs to the process. For example, the owner of the process 'Develop new products' can continue to develop weird and wonderful things that nobody wants if there is no clear definition of what new products are required. This definition would normally come from outside this process (unless the 'Develop new products' process is defined as *including* the specification of requirements as a *subprocess*, of course). Equally, a superbly equipped and staffed education centre can be running otherwise excellent education programmes, except that the people so educated do not meet the needs of the enterprise. Nobody has told the manager in charge what exactly are the skills required for the future.

Because they originate beyond the boundaries of the process, these essential inputs must be negotiated by the process owner. And negotiation for them cannot begin until:

1 the needed inputs have been decided

2 the suppliers of these inputs have been identified.

At top management level, the vast majority of inputs needed for a process are in the form of information. There is almost no movement of physical entities at this level of management. Now that there is a clear definition of the process future desired state, each process owner should be able to decide precisely what inputs are essential to assure its accomplishment.

The process owners are recommended to take a thoroughly selfish view about this, to consider *only* what the needs of *their* process (or processes) are — *all* of the needs. Forget about external customers of the process, at this stage.

This self-centred approach may appear to be contradictory in a study that claims to be so customer- and competitor-focused, but each process future desired state has been framed with the customer's needs in mind. These needs, which will also serve to make the enterprise more competitive, are deeply embedded in the corresponding need for improvements in processes, because they were central to the definition of the future desired states of the business processes. Accomplishing these will depend on complete and excellent inputs.

Equally, process owners should ignore what may be presumed to be the needs of *internal* customers of the process. These needs will be very clearly identified, soon.

Each member of Doppler's management team works individually now, deciding the necessary inputs for their process or processes, focusing intently on the need to accomplish their particular process future desired state.

For example, the owner of 'Monitor the competition' produced the following.

Process:	**Monitor the competition**
Future desired state:	**On a day-by-day basis, we are fully aware of the strengths and weaknesses of all our competitors, their current position in the market and their strategies for the future.**
Essential inputs:	**Who are our competitors?**
	Where are they operating?
	What is in their product range?
	What are their prices?
	What is selling well? Why?
	What is not selling well? Why?
	What are their individual market shares
	How have they changed?
	Who are their key suppliers?
	How do they like doing business with our competitors?
	What is our competitors' management style/ quality?
	What are their preferred selling methods?

> What is their organization's structure?
> Who are their key people?
> Cash flows? Financial strengths/weaknesses?
> Personnel strengths? Weaknesses?
> Any morale issues, etc.?
> What are customers' perceptions of our competitors?
> Why do they buy what they buy from competitors?
> What do they complain about to competitors and to us about competitors?
> Are there any special relationships with government bodies, Members of Parliament, and so on?
> How do we and they stand in financial markets?
> What is media's coverage of them and us?

In contrast, the owner of 'Order products for stores' produced the following.

Process:	**Order products for stores**
Future desired state:	**We know so much about our customers that we always have cost-effective availability of products.**
Essential inputs:	**What are customers buying from us and from the competition?**
	What do they complain to us about?
	Why do they buy?
	When do they buy? How often?
	What is in our product range now, next month?
	What is selling well? Why? Where?
	What is not selling well? Why?
	What are the different stores' characteristics — geographic, ethnic, demographic, cultural?
	What are we advertising? How effective is it?
	What is in stock in the stores and in the warehouses?
	What is in the pipeline from suppliers?
	When will it arrive at the warehouses?

These examples are not meant to be complete. You could no doubt think of some important omissions from these two lists. But if you were doing this for your *own* business process, for which there was a clearly defined future desired state, then it would be complete, no doubt.

It took about an hour to decide what the essential inputs for each process were if it was to be able to accomplish its future desired state. After the process owners had worked individually, they presented their findings to their colleagues, who were able to discuss them and suggest possible additions to the lists.

Now that the essential inputs had been decided for each most critical process, the owners could then turn to answering Question 6, 'Who are the suppliers of necessary inputs?'

10

The suppliers of essential process inputs

Doppler Electronics' top management team were now within about two hours of being able to make a complete, strategic model of their business, that is, the way it *should* be to '... maximize the Total Competitiveness of Doppler Electronics', their future desired state, which was agreed just the morning before. This model will show all of the essential relationships between their most critical business processes, that is, the necessary connections between the processes, *and what will have to flow between them* — mostly, information. They will have a complete, internal supplier-to-process-to-customer model for their most critical business processes. This will be a useful contribution to finding business re-engineering opportunities, later. And it can all be traced back along the thread to the enterprise's future desired state.

First, though, they needed to identify the suppliers of essential inputs to each of the most critical processes they had defined. Then, building the model is easy.

There are two major categories of supplier: those within the enterprise (internal suppliers), and those external to it.

There is a subcategory of external suppliers that it is useful to identify separately when the enterprise is a business unit, say, of a large corporation or a group. If such suppliers are outside of the enterprise but within the corporation or group, call them 'quasi-external suppliers'.

Such suppliers are not wholly external, and they are certainly not within the scope of the business unit doing the study, but

113

they may be among the most difficult with whom to negotiate, particularly if negotiation across geographic, cultural, and linguistic boundaries is involved, and when converging career paths might get in the way.

The example of the future desired state for the process 'Negotiate product supplies' in Table 8.1 illustrates the point. This example came from a European subsidiary of a global US based corporation. The process was totally at the mercy of the people in the United States as they supplied the products — there was no other source of product supplies. Yet, the European subsidiary was doing all of the good things of marketing and so on and was taking some important orders from customers. When there was an urgent need for products in the United States, this took priority over the European subsidiary's orders. The impact this had on customer satisfaction in Europe can easily be imagined.

It is also useful to distinguish quasi-external *customers* from truly external ones. Some of the most important stakeholders in the European subsidiary mentioned above were quasi-external customers in the United States. *They* were depending on the outputs (such as money) of their European subsidiary as a whole. If a supplier is also a customer (a common situation), then you are in a much stronger position to negotiate your essential inputs, particularly if the quality and quantity of the inputs are prejudicing the quality of the outputs. This point was not lost on the Chief Executive of the European subsidiary, nor on the owner of the 'Negotiate product supply' process.

In any top-management team, most of the key suppliers are internal; fellow owners of most critical business processes. Because we need a full understanding of the mutual dependencies of the processes, *internal suppliers are identified by the name of the process*, not the name of the individual; not the function; not the job title.

So, the owner of 'Order products for stores', for example, has a list of potential *internal* suppliers that relate only to the other

114

ten most critical business processes, namely:

- Define market strategies
- Procure products
- Order products for warehouses
- Merchandize products
- Monitor competition
- Monitor product quality
- Monitor customer complaints
- Review technology opportunities
- Identify/cultivate relationships with key opinion formers
- Monitor personnel motivation.

The owner scrutinized the list of essential inputs — those that enable the process to accomplish its future desired state — then identified the internal suppliers of any of these inputs by the name of the process on the above list.

Sometimes an essential input may be identified that has to come from within the enterprise, but does not naturally originate within one of the processes on this short, rather exclusive list. It may originate within a process that is not even on the Critical Success Factor/process matrix, such as 'Pay personnel', or from within a function, such as the General Ledger Department.

In this case, the owner of 'Order products for stores' knows which *colleague* has responsibility for payroll or general ledger. The owner *should* know — there are only eight people in total, after all. This colleague owns at least one of the processes on the list of most critical business processes — it could be 'Procure products' or 'Monitor the competition', anything. It does not matter. The name of the colleague's *process* is still specified as the key supplier, even though the specific information (say, from the general ledger) may not originate within the critical *process* of which that colleague is owner. The essential general ledger input has to be negotiated with the 'owner' of it, who now also happens to be the owner of a critical business process. It is the key process-to-process relationships that have to be revealed, and that means the owner-to-owner relationships. That is where the negotiation has to take place, after all. Alternatively, you can make an additional classification of suppliers of these inputs which do *not* originate within the list of most critical processes, identifying them by the name of the colleague concerned. The end result will be the same.

However, the owners of processes will usually find that the majority of their needed inputs lie within the other most critical business processes. If in doubt, ask.

External suppliers of essential inputs are identified by generic type, or the name of a particular enterprise, such as:

- component manufacturers
- office equipment manufacturers
- advertising agencies
- graphics studios
- market research organizations
- political lobbyists
- standards organizations
- the European Parliament
- public relations consultants
- management consultants
- the media
- translation services
- suppliers of raw materials
- software houses
- oil companies
- investigation agencies
- the European Space Agency
- travel agents
- conference organizers
- and so forth.

The owner of 'Order products for stores' produced the following list of suppliers, distinguishing between internal and external suppliers.

Process:	**Order products for stores**
Internal suppliers:	**The owners of the following processes:**
	• **Procure products**
	• **Order products for warehouses**
	• **Merchandize products**
	• **Monitor the competition**
	• **Monitor product quality**
	• **Monitor customer complaints**
External suppliers:	**Advertising agents**
	Market research organizations
	The media
	Census data

For each supplier listed, the owner of 'Order products for stores' was then able to say precisely which essential inputs would originate from them.

The owner of the 'Monitor the competition' process produced a list like this.

Process:	**Monitor the competition**
Internal suppliers:	**The owners of the following processes:**
	• **Define market strategies**
	• **Procure products**
	• **Merchandize products**
	• **Monitor customer complaints**
	• **Identify/cultivate relationships with key opinion formers**
	• **Monitor personnel motivation**
External suppliers:	**Advertising agencies**
	Market research organizations
	Public relations consultants
	Political lobbyists
	The media
	'Contacts'

Again, the owner of this process was able to say exactly which essential inputs would come from each supplier. As might be expected, there are rather more external suppliers to this process than there were for the 'order products for stores' process (and note that the above list of external suppliers is not complete).

Now it is possible to see why the owners of the processes were encouraged to take a totally selfish view of their needs and to ignore their internal customers.

Consider the internal suppliers of the 'Monitor the competition' process. One of them is 'Merchandize products'. It was chosen because this process is the source of something needed by the owner of 'Monitor the competition'. From the perspective of the owner of the 'Merchandize products' process, then, the owner of 'Monitor the competition' is a key *customer* — if you are my supplier, then I am your customer.

The owner of the 'Order products for stores' process has *also* listed the 'Merchandize products' process as a key *supplier*, perhaps for a totally different set of necessary inputs. As soon as the owner of 'Merchandize products' sees these two lists, it is clear that this owner has at least two, key internal *customers*:

- 'Monitor the competition'
- 'Order products for stores'

because the owners of both of them independently identified 'Merchandize products' as a key *supplier*. The owner of 'Merchandize products' has two key customers now, whether that owner likes it or not. And there may be more internal customers when all of the answers to the question 'Who are your key internal suppliers?' have been assembled. Moreover, the answers to Question 5, 'What are the inputs needed for each critical process?' reveal what is needed to flow from the 'Merchandize products' process to those two (maybe more) key internal customers.

The next chapter describes how to assemble all of this information to create the internal supplier-to-process-to-customer model of Doppler's most critical business processes. Now the suppliers have been identified, we have all the necessary information to do this. It will be a highly revealing view of what the mutual needs of the most critical business processes are if they are to accomplish their individual, and the enterprise's, future desired state. It will also be a rich source of material for innovative thinking, and the raw information required for effective allocation of resources, organization design, and for business re-engineering. It represents the valuable prize at this end of the thread, the justification for the effort of answering the first six apparently simple and logically connected questions.

The majority of the opportunities that exist to become more competitive, to start re-engineering projects, and so forth, will be found there. To find the rest of the opportunities, we need the answers to Question 7, which looks *inside* each of the most critical business processes. This question is discussed in Chapter 12.

11

The internal supplier-to-process-to-customer matrix

It is worth following the thread back once more to see how the Doppler team arrived at this point, the point at which they can build, through a series of steps, the process-to-process model of their company.

Their all-important
↓
Future desired state
↓
has been the source of their
↓
Critical Success Factors
↓
which were the means of identifying their
↓
most critical business processes
↓
from which they derived the
↓
future desired states of these processes
↓
which enabled them to determine what were their
↓
essential inputs
↓

120

so that they could identify their
↓
internal and external suppliers.

In this chapter, we shall be building a matrix that will show all of the key process-to-process connections. It is important to note that this matrix has absolutely no connection with the Critical Success Factor/process matrix that was used earlier to find the most critical business processes. The new matrix has the most critical business processes down the left-hand side, but the resemblance ends there.

Figure 11.1 shows how the matrix is constructed. The most critical business processes are listed down the left-hand side, not in order of priority. Consider the process 'order products for stores'. It is fourth on the list. It has a letter 'P' in the fourth column, which identifies this column as belonging to the process 'Order products for stores'. In the same way, 'Monitor the competition', the sixth process on the list, has a 'P' in the sixth column, and so on.

Now, we simply transfer the list of internal suppliers identified by the owner of 'Order products for stores' to its vertical column on the matrix. Its internal suppliers are the owners of the processes:

- Procure products
- Order products for warehouses
- Merchandize products
- Monitor the competition
- Monitor product quality
- Monitor customer complaints.

An 'S' is placed in the vertical column belonging to 'Order products for stores' against each process listed as an internal supplier.

121

Most critical business processes

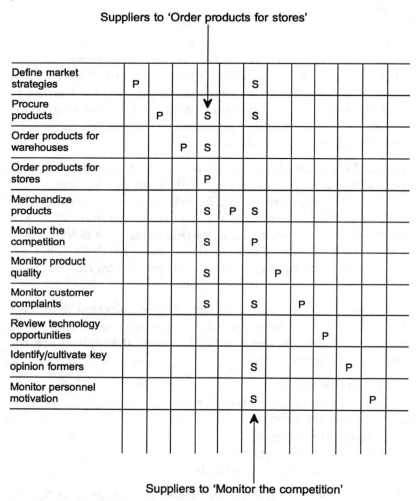

Figure 11.1 Part of Doppler Electronics' matrix of internal supplier-to-process connections

The owner of the 'Monitor the competition' process, you will recall, identified a different set of internal suppliers, namely:

- Define market strategies
- Procure products
- Merchandize products
- Monitor customer complaints
- Identify/cultivate relationships with key opinion formers
- Monitor personnel motivation.

Again, these are identified by the 'S's against the name of each supplier process in the vertical column belonging to 'Monitor the competition', indicated by the 'P' across from its entry on the left-hand side. Simple!

When the same thing was done for all the remaining most critical business processes identified by Doppler's team, the result was the matrix shown in Figure 11.2. Thus, all the internal suppliers for each of the most critical business processes are displayed on one small piece of paper.

So, to find out which internal suppliers are needed by any one process, you only have to look for the 'S's in the vertical column belonging to that process. For example, the owner of 'Order products for warehouses' can quickly be seen to have identified only two internal suppliers, namely:

- Procure products
- Order products for stores.

In contrast, the owner of the 'Monitor personnel motivation' process has obviously identified that the process has a critical need for something from every other most critical business process — all of them have an 'S' in the vertical column belonging to this process. Clearly, we now have displayed all of the supplier-to-process relationships for Doppler Electronics that are critical to its accomplishing its Critical Success Factors, and thereby, its future desired state. In the case of this company, this means that the necessary information — and anything else — must flow along those supplier-to-process connections to enable each of the process owners to

123

Define market strategies	P	S			S	S			S	S	S
Procure products	S	P	S	S	S	S	S		S		S
Order products for warehouses			P	S							S
Order products for stores			S	P							S
Merchandize products	S			S	P	S		S			S
Monitor the competition	S	S		S	S	P	S	S	S	S	S
Monitor product quality		S		S	S		P				S
Monitor customer complaints	S	S		S	S	S	S	P	S	S	S
Review technology opportunities	S				S		S	S	P	S	S
Identify/cultivate key opinion formers	S	S				S			S	P	S
Monitor personnel motivation					S	S	S			S	P

Figure 11.2 Doppler Electronics' internal supplier-to-process-to-customer matrix

maximize Doppler Electronics' Total Competitiveness, individually and collectively.

Now, here's the magic bit. All of Doppler's internal process-to-*customer* relationships are also displayed on the matrix, even though they were not directly sought. They follow from the simple logic expressed in the last chapter: 'If you are my supplier, then I am your customer'. Therefore, the following is true:

- the *supplier*-to-*process* relationships are shown in the vertical columns — this is how the matrix was constructed
- The *process*-to-*customer* relationships are revealed by the *horizontal rows*.

Consider the 'Order products for stores' process again. There are two 'S's in its horizontal row. This means that this process has two internal customers, *whether its owner likes it or not* — the owner did not select them as customers. Rather, the owners of two other processes selected 'Order products for stores' as a key *supplier*.

Now, we can find out the identities of the two key internal customers of the 'Order products for stores' process. The first 'S' in its horizontal row is just to the left of its 'P'. And we know that an 'S' means that some other process owner identified 'Order products for stores' as a key supplier. Who? It was the owner of the 'Order products for warehouses' process, because this 'S' is in the vertical column that belongs to 'Order products for warehouses'. This was how the matrix was made.

We can find the second key internal customer of 'Order products for stores' in the same way. The second 'S' in the horizontal row for 'Order products for stores' is at the right-hand side. It is there because the owner of 'Monitor personnel motivation' identified 'Order products for stores' as a key supplier. The 'S' is in the vertical column belonging to 'Monitor personnel motivation'. Therefore, from the perspective of the owner of 'Order products for stores', the owner of 'Monitor personnel motivation' is a key *customer*.

So, the matrix not only shows the *suppliers* identified by the owner of the 'Order products for stores' process, it also reveals that the owner has two key internal *customers*, namely:

- Order products for warehouses
- Monitor personnel motivation.

And we can do the same thing for any of the other processes, of course.

The owner of the 'Order products for stores' process not only must negotiate the inputs needed for this process, from the identified suppliers, but also be prepared to negotiate with the owners of its internal customer processes. They *also* have a critical (and different) need for inputs.

Figure 11.3 shows a model of this situation for the two most critical processes we have been looking at — 'Order products for stores' and 'Order products for warehouses', with all of their essential supplier-to-process-to-customer connections. Notice that these were both derived simply by asking all of the owners of the process to identify their key *suppliers*, knowing their essential inputs. Soon we shall be joining all of these individual models of the processes together to get the holistic view of Doppler's most critical business processes and their mutual dependencies.

'Cinderella' business processes

The supplier-to-process-to-customer matrix reveals even more.

Consider the process 'Monitor customer complaints', for example (see Figure 11.2.) There are nine 'S's in its horizontal row, so it has nine other most critical business processes as its internal customers (this is a very typical pattern for this process in commercial organizations today, by the way). Each of these processes, owned by a colleague, has a critical need for information from 'Monitor customer complaints'. All nine of them identified this process as being a supplier of inputs essential to take *their* processes to states of competitive excellence.

How much does the process 'Monitor customer complaints' normally get in terms of resources? The answer, in most enterprises, is approximately zero; the case of General Electric described earlier is relatively rare. However, now, as a result of answering these six questions, the owners of nine of Doppler Electronics' most critical business processes will soon be converging on the owner of 'Monitor customer complaints' to define their needs. And they are genuine needs, which

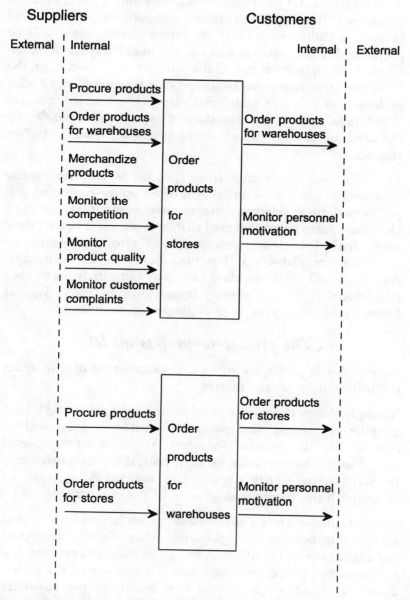

Figure 11.3 Model of the internal suppliers and customers for two of Doppler Electronics' critical business processes

must be satisfied. Otherwise, nine of the most critical business processes will be unable to achieve competitive excellence and Doppler's ability to achieve its future desired state will be prejudiced. (This process also has a primary impact on seven Critical Success Factors.) Quite quickly, the owner of the 'Monitor customer complaints' process is going to need a lot of help and a lot of additional resources to transform this 'Cinderella' process into the state of excellence demanded by the needs of its internal customers. Perhaps it needs to be 're-engineered'?

The 'Monitor the competition' process is another typical 'Cinderella' process — one that is often under-resourced and performed in a relatively fragmented way, if at all. Yet, Doppler's team has discovered that, not only is it one of their most critical business processes, but also, like 'Monitor customer complaints', it has nine key internal customers. And they will be demanding excellent outputs from it, too. (Additionally, it has a primary impact on six Critical Success Factors.) Another process re-engineering candidate?

The process-to-process model

Figure 11.4 is perhaps a more convenient way of displaying the information on the matrix.

It simply shows the most critical business processes and all the supplier-to-process and process-to-customer relationships revealed by the matrix. In effect, this is a strategic-level model of the business, for its most critical business processes, to satisfy the needs of the top management team to accomplish the future desired state of the enterprise.

A solid line with an arrowhead at each end indicates a relationship between two processes where each is a supplier *and* a customer of the other. A dotted line shows a relationship between two processes where one is a *customer* of the other. The arrowhead of the dotted lines points to the customer process. All of this was derived from Doppler's supplier-to-process-to-customer matrix.

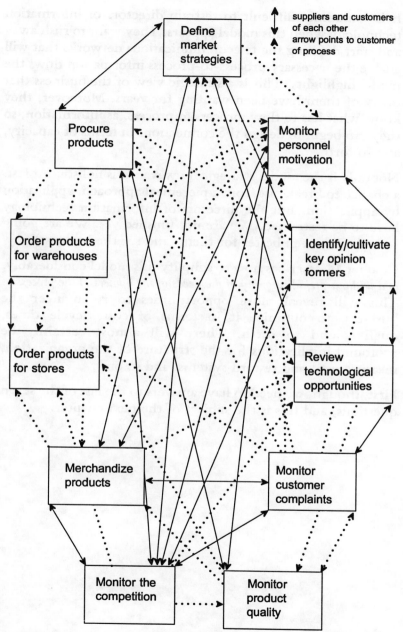

suppliers and customers
of each other
arrow points to customer
of process

Figure 11.4 Process–to–process business model for Doppler Electronics

129

It is sometimes difficult to restrain directors of information technology when this model appears. They want to rush away and start defining the telecommunications networks that will enable the necessary process-to-process information flows the model highlights. This is a strategic view of the business that many of them have been wanting for years. Moreover, they know what has to flow, process to process, as information, so they can begin to design the connections in terms of capacity, and so forth.

Not only is the model strategic, however, it is holistic. At last, a chance to break out from a piecemeal approach, application by application! But the directors of information technology have to be restrained. We are not finished yet. We are going to make life even better for them (and for the business).

Chapter 14 describes how to simplify this model considerably, *and without prejudicing any of the needs of the owners of the processes.* This will reveal more opportunities to re-engineer the business, to optimize it in terms of costs, cycle times, quality, and so forth. There will almost certainly be profound implications for the structure of the organization, measurement and reward systems, and so on.

First, though, we need to have answers to the last of the seven questions, and this is the subject of the next chapter.

12

The internal structure of the most critical business processes

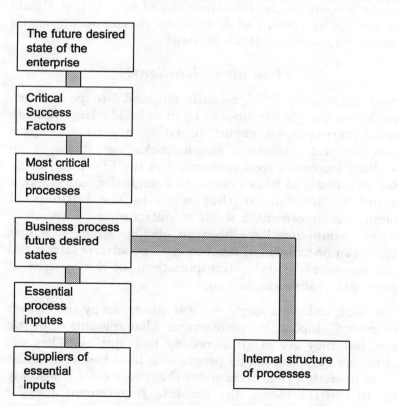

The future desired state of the enterprise

Critical Success Factors

Most critical business processes

Business process future desired states

Essential process inputes

Suppliers of essential inputs

Internal structure of processes

Figure 12.1 A separate strand of the thread that connects all the steps taken so far

131

This is a separate strand of the thread that has run through all the steps taken so far, (see Figure 12.1). It leads directly from Question 4, 'What is the future desired state of each critical process?' Of course, its origin still lies within the enterprise's future desired state.

Here, we look inside each process to find the optimum way of organizing it internally. The first question to ask is, 'Where will the process be performed?'

As usual, the answer to this should be derived from consideration of the future desired state of the process or the enterprise. If in doubt, refer again to the definition of Total Competitiveness/Effectiveness and ask, 'Where should the process be performed to have the maximum impact on Total Competitiveness/Effectiveness?'

How many locations?

The French group BSN, recently renamed Groupe Danone, has chosen a single site close to Lyon to build a large plant to manufacture enough yogurt to satisfy a market of pan-European scale. Modern, aseptic packaging, access to an excellent European road network, and the European Single Market influenced BSN's choice of a single site, and where it should be located. If they were in the business of manufacturing cement, a single manufacturing site for all of Europe would not have been an obvious strategy, but as yogurt can be handled in this way with no adverse effects and with reasonable costs of transportation, all the benefits of economies of scale can be taken.

A decision to have a single site was also taken by the Danish company Coloplast. It manufactures what amounts to plastic bags, but they are of an incredibly high quality. They are colostomy bags, needed by people who have had a particular bowel operation that necessitates them to wear a colostomy bag thereafter. Hence the absolute requirement for the highest possible quality.

Coloplast exports 98 per cent of what it manufactures in Denmark. This means it has relatively high distribution costs, the penalty for manufacturing in one site for a global market. Of course, it benefits from considerable economies of scale that accrue from operating from a single site, which BSN valued, but this was not the reason behind Coloplast's decision — and Danish workers are not the cheapest labour force in the world either.

At first glance, it might be supposed that good plastic bags could be made anywhere. The raw material is polyolefin film, which is readily available in a large number of places. However, it was the need for superb quality that drove Coloplast's decision to operate from a single site. To achieve such consistently high quality, it designs its own machinery and manufacturing processes. If Coloplast were to proliferate the process 'Manufacture products', it would become very difficult to retain the proprietary knowledge about the process that produces such competitively high-quality products. Coloplast's decision to perform the process in one place is therefore the same as the French Group Danone's — the decisions were taken to maximize their competitiveness. What exactly made each company more competitive was quite different, however.

In the case of Doppler Electronics, the management team may decide that the process 'order products for warehouses', for example, would best be performed in one, central location, close to good road and rail transport. On the other hand, it may decide that the impact on Total Competitiveness would be higher if the company had, say, three regional warehouses in the United Kingdom. As usual, there are trade-offs to be made in terms of costs and customer service. Doppler Electronics *did* have three regional warehouses, at that time, and decided that this was right, for the moment.

How much coordination between locations?

As soon as it is decided that a business process will be performed in more than one location, a second question must be answered: 'What level of coupling is appropriate between the different locations?'

'Appropriate' is meant in terms of achieving the future desired state or maximizing Total Competitiveness/Effectiveness. (Obviously, if the process is performed in only one place, the question of internal coupling does not arise.) Figure 12.2. shows a useful way in which to model the answers to this last question.

The French Group Danone has decided to position the process 'Manufacture products' (in the case of yogurt) in the bottom left-hand corner, for good strategic reasons, from its perspective. The Danish company Coloplast is obviously in

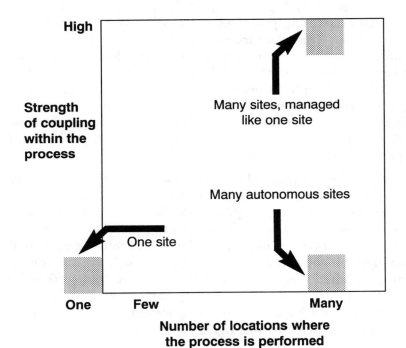

Figure 12.2   Model of answers to the question 'What is the competitive internal structure of each critical process?'

the same place in the diagram — it has one location, therefore, there is no internal coupling — for the same process 'Manufacture products', but for totally different strategic reasons. Both may be wrong, but it is their decision.

In contrast, the 'company credo' of Johnson and Johnson — lots of local autonomy — meant that 'Manufacture products' would be located in the bottom-right of the diagram, corresponding to multiple sites with, effectively, little or no coordination.

Cummins Engines is positioned in the top-right for the process 'Manufacture products'. It makes diesel engines in a number of plants round the world. The globally dispersed plants are so tightly coupled, the effect is as though they are all located behind the same boundary fence.

Looking back to General Electric's process 'Monitor customer complaints', we can see that it would be located in the bottom-left corner — it *all* happens in Louisville, Kentucky — but there are many connections *from* the process to other internal GE processes and to processes beyond GE, to its dealers and agents.

Doppler's team had to answer this question, not only for the process 'Order products for warehouses', but also for every other most critical business process that is performed in more than one location. They found it helpful to structure their answers by using a simple scale like this:

1 = tightly coupled — do everything this way
2 = strong coordination — do these things these ways
3 = medium coordination — follow these standards
4 = mild coordination — follow these guidelines
5 = hands off — do it your way.

It was decided that there should be strong coordination regarding the 'Order products for warehouses' (scoring '2' on the above scale) between the three locations where it is performed. On the other hand, they decided that the 'Procure products' process would be done centrally, in one location, to enable more effective negotiation with the major suppliers of consumer electronics products. A glance at the process-to-process model of the business on page 129 shows the connections *between* these two processes (and also to other processes, such as 'Order products for stores', of course).

Now, with a knowledge of the strategic requirements for coupling *within* each process, as well as the requirements for coupling *between* each process, the Director of the Information Technology Department was even better equipped to think about telecommunications and data management issues, and so forth.

The Doppler Electronics' management team had now answered all seven of the questions. They had all the raw material available to challenge the status quo and to look for the most important re-engineering opportunities, as well as for simpler projects for increasing their Total Competitiveness.

It was the evening of the second day of their study, the formal part of which was now finished. The rest of the work would have to be done 'back at the ranch', so to speak.

'We have made history. Now let's have dinner.'
Camillo Cavour, on the end of the Italian Risorgimento, 23 April 1859.

Part 4

SELECTING THE OPPORTUNITIES FOR COMPETITIVENESS

Introduction

The word 'competitiveness' is used deliberately in the title of Part 4 rather than 'business re-engineering'. Often, many opportunities will be revealed that can be exploited quickly, do not come within the definition of re-engineering, but *can* have a big impact on Total Competitiveness/Effectiveness.

Many examples will be given of enterprises that have increased their competitiveness (there are even more in the Appendix at the end of this book). In each case, it was never simply the result of good luck or clever technology. Most of the examples given did rely on the use of information technology and telecommunications, but the distinguishing feature between the winners and the losers is what happens in the *brains* of their people, rather than in their *computers* — the same technology, after all, is available to everyone. Computer salesmen do not discriminate between buyers.

This need for brains rather than clever computing is borne out by some comparisons made between Japanese and European companies in the use of 'concurrent engineering'. In simple terms, this is the 'develop new products' process when all the involved business processes, in the company as well as its suppliers and customers, operate together in cross-functional teams. It can extend right through to the manufacture and launching of a new product.

A survey in the UK by PA Consulting found that only a quarter of the 70 firms questioned were beyond the initial stages of implementation. A major reason is that concurrent engineering involves major organizational changes, not only internally, but also along the whole supply chain. It sounds like a case of re-engineering.

Of 30 major Japanese manufacturers studied, 70 per cent were practising concurrent engineering, without any sophisticated information technology. In contrast, most UK manufacturers have the technology, *but many still have inappropriate processes.*

13

Big bang or softly, softly?

The answers to the seven questions provide a rich source of opportunities to improve Total Competitiveness/Effectiveness. The sheer size and number of opportunities can present a dilemma to the top management team: 'Where do we start?', 'How much do we start with?', 'What should we do after that?'

The big bang approach

The ultimate response is to put in place all the necessary resources, the computer technology, the internal and process-to-process telecommunications, and so on; restructure the enterprise; provide the necessary education and training; and whatever else is needed to support each process owner in achieving the individual and collective future desired states. We can call this the big bang approach. Few existing enterprises would make this choice. It can take time — measured in years — to put even the necessary telecommunications networks in place. Meanwhile, the target may have moved, new competitors appeared, new technologies, new market opportunities. (It is for this reason that the enterprise's future desired state and Critical Success Factors should be revisited every 12 months or so, to keep the enterprise in tune with its environment. The necessary changes may be small, but important.)

If a big bang approach *could* be implemented in a short time, say, less than a year, it would be splendid, of course. Any necessary subsequent changes would then be made to a collectively excellent and highly adaptive enterprise. But such an aggressive timetable is too short and the cost and risks are too high for most enterprises to swallow. Nevertheless, the journey towards maximizing Total Competitiveness/Effectiveness should start as soon as possible. Any needed changes will then be made to something that, while not yet perfect, is already better and more adaptive than it was.

A big bang approach may be appropriate for an entirely new enterprise, however. Here, there is *no* internal status quo to be challenged, only the entrenched attitudes and status quo of the existing competitors. The UK's Midland Bank's subsidiary First Direct, illustrates this approach (Midland was taken over by the Hong Kong and Shanghai Banking Corporation in 1992). The Midland's existing branch network was effectively left in place while First Direct was designed from scratch.

Inventing a new kind of bank

There are no First Direct branches. The entire bank was developed around the concept of 24-hour availability, every day of the year. Customers access the bank by telephone. A First Direct banking representative handles the customer's call and can conduct an extensive set of financial transactions, from a simple balance update to organizing a personal loan or a mortgage. Customers of First Direct can obtain cash from a network of more than 7000 bank cash machines in the UK, and they can cash cheques free of charge at Midland branches.

The bank was launched on 1 October 1989, a Sunday. Since then, it has experienced excellent growth. *Three-quarters of its current depositors are defectors from competitor banks.* By September 1992, it had an account base of 300 000. By June 1993, it had more than 400 000 customers. Then, it had to stop advertising to try to stem the tide of new customers, because of fears that the quality of customer service might deteriorate (but as a third of its business came from recommendations, this could only ever have been partially effective). It was necessary to hire 400 extra staff to prevent its systems from being overloaded. So becoming more competitive does not necessarily mean 'downsizing'!

First Direct expects to have around 20 per cent of an expected UK market of 6 million telephone banking accounts by the year 2000. Perhaps more important, it is seen as a possible prototype by its owners, the Hong Kong and Shanghai Banking Corporation, the world's twelfth largest bank, with assets of $258 billion in 1993.

141

First Direct was not so much '*re*-engineered as 'engineered' properly in the first place for its time and its environment. But, nevertheless, it provides an exemplar for the *principles* of re-engineering, with its big challenge to the status quo of retail banking. About 25 years ago, probably the only way a new competitor could take on the long-established high street banks of the United Kingdom was to match them, at least, in the number and excellence of their branch networks. This would have represented a huge start-up cost in expensive property and expensive people. This is a very high barrier to competitive entry. Today, information technology and telecommunications, plus a more technically aware and receptive market-place (50 per cent of First Direct's customers are in the 18 to 34 age bracket) have effectively removed these barriers to entry.

As a re-engineering exemplar, we can learn more from the First Direct case. There is a large investment in personnel education and training, and re-training. No banking representative recruit is allowed any telephone contact with a customer before a minimum of six weeks of intensive training have been completed. Moreover, the representatives are selected on the basis of customer service skills. They come from a wide variety of backgrounds. The general ethos is that all staff really value their relationship with the customer, in direct contrast with the more traditional, 'It's more than my job's worth!' mentality. This extends to an open-plan working environment, located in Leeds, in the North of England. Senior managers do have partitioned areas — for practical as opposed to status reasons — but there are no closed offices and no doors to close. This is a culture unique in British Banking, where it is still common for staff to refer to superiors as Mr, Mrs or Miss, where managers are usually segregated from their staff by separate offices on separate floors, and where staff are expected to approach management only through the person directly above them in the hierarchy.

Inventing a new market

Federal Express is another example of a big bang approach. Its chairman, Frederick W. Smith more or less invented the market for delivering packages overnight in the United States, with guaranteed delivery next day. Late delivery, and the customer does not pay. Now, Federal Express is a global business with its own fleet of aircraft and delivery vans on-line to its central computing systems.

Fred Smith started the business with an $8 million legacy. It grew to be a $1 billion business in less than 10 years.

The entire business depends upon sophisticated information technology and telecommunications services that enable a customer's package to be tracked at all stages of its journey. The system is called COSMOS.

Hand-held terminals enable drivers to compile customer data at the point of collection. Terminals in their vans are linked directly to Federal Express mainframe computers (in 1989, Federal Express was IBM's tenth biggest customer; the first nine were all government customers). This direct connection between vans and the mainframe computers reduces mistakes in routing packages, among other things. It also allows drivers to spot delinquent accounts, thereby reducing the amount of bad debt that has to be written off.

Federal Express became so good, through its sophisticated tracking system, it became a Just-In-Time middle man. It manages inventories of high-priced goods at its various sorting hubs. For example, it has a contract with the UK fashion and furnishings group, Laura Ashley, to handle all of Laura Ashley's logistics. It has a similar deal with National Semiconductor, the US computer chip company, to set up and operate the distribution network for National Semiconductor's Asian subsidiaries. The aim is to cut down the time between placing an order and its delivery, currently between 7 and 21 days, to a maximum of 4.

The COSMOS investment was a big bang approach. No single part of it could work until it was *all* in place. It needed the single-minded drive from the top and the correspondingly high financial as well as project management investments to ensure its success. And, like Midland Bank's First Direct, it was *not* a re-engineering project — it happened before the term was invented — but it has all of the key characteristics of business re-engineering: fundamental re-thinking; a radical approach; and a focus on the key processes to achieve dramatic results. Moreover, the excellence of its own critical business processes has enabled Federal Express to generate new and profitable revenue streams that *depend* upon the excellence of its core business processes.

The softly, softly approach — one process

There is a continuous range of opportunities, all the way from big bang down to selecting only one of the most critical business processes and making it competitively excellent. The latter approach carries the smaller risk, and a correspondingly smaller return. Nevertheless, it is an appropriate way to get started for many management teams. The change from managing functions to managing cross-functional business processes is a very large one. A lot of valuable learning will result from improving just *one* critical process to competitive excellence.

If this approach is taken, it is essential that the entire management team accepts the implications of their collective work in answering the seven key questions, *insofar as the chosen process is concerned*. This means that the rest of the team must not turn their backs on the owner of the chosen process and go back to business as usual. Usually, not all of the owner's colleagues will be internal suppliers, but those who are suppliers of necessary inputs must be prepared to provide the process owner with whatever is needed to accomplish its future desired state. And its internal customers must be ready to define *their* requirements clearly. (This, in turn, may lead to a renegotiation of some of the process inputs.)

The process will almost certainly need additional resources. These will probably include quite significant investments in information technology and telecommunications. The team approach to answering the seven key questions should ensure the backing of all colleagues for the selected process owner in any necessary reallocation of limited resources. Their two to three days of work together thus far should also have

144

convinced all of the management team that this first process improvement project is no mere experiment. Its purpose is to gain knowledge. It is the pilot project that will show the way in which the entire enterprise can be transformed by moving *all* the most critical business processes towards their future desired states. This is just the first step along a committed journey to competitive excellence. The consequences of *not* continuing are just as clear to all members of the team as are the revealed opportunities, which they themselves have just discovered.

If this pilot approach is taken, focusing on just one of the most critical business processes, it is essential that the right process is chosen. This must be up to the management team, perhaps with the CEO having the final say. There are no hard-and-fast rules for choosing the right process; trade-offs will have to be made between different factors. These might include the following.

- *Urgency* Is there a single process the current performance of which is so bad that it represents a severe threat to the enterprise? This will normally be clearly recognized and acknowledged by all members of the team. Figure 7.4 (see page 84), which was used to identify Doppler's most critical business processes, may be useful in the selection of just one process. Doppler's Process 11 has the highest score in terms of impact on the Critical Success Factors (quality is D, bad, and it impacts seven Critical Success Factors). This is the process 'Monitor customer complaints'.
- *Timescale* How long will it take to accomplish success, to improve the process to competitive excellence? If it will take five years, then this is too long. As a pilot project, it is better to choose something that will be successful relatively quickly.
- *Impact on the organization* How large are any of the changes to the structure of the organization necessary to ensure success? The softly, softly approach suggests avoiding projects that will involve massive structural changes. Equally, avoid something that is so stand-alone that the organization's status quo is not challenged (this is unlikely,

145

by the way). Organizational learning should be an important component of the pilot project. Much bigger changes will follow.

- *Technical risk* This can be very enterprise-specific. If the project requires the use of leading-edge technologies, particularly if they are technologies with which your own personnel have no experience, it may be better to choose something else. This project is too important to risk failure by using exotic technologies.
- *Size of the project* Large, complicated projects are famous for being delivered late, incomplete, and costing significantly more than was initially forecast. Keep it small enough to enable it to be closely managed, scrutinized, and controlled.

In essence, it has to be something that will provide a significant amount of learning, which means that it must not be trivially simple, but that must be a resounding success, relatively soon. The fact that it results from the process of answering the seven key questions should ensure that it is not a dead-end project.

Functional triumph: lost opportunity

The experience of Allied Dunbar, a financial services organization in the UK, shows what can happen if a blinkered, functional approach is taken.

Allied Dunbar bought 3500 Toshiba laptop personal computers for its sales representatives. The computers contained some specially written software that supported the sales representatives in a question-and-answer session with a customer or prospect — age, marital status, earnings, number of children, educational plans, financial status, investments, insurance cover, and so forth. The computer could then perform a 'financial health check' of the customer, showing areas of potential exposure and, naturally, offering opportunities to invest in Allied Dunbar's range of financial products.

It was an outstanding success. New sales representatives with the personal computer were developing up to four times as much business as experienced representatives without one. In effect, the

---

process 'Offer products for sale' was being considerably improved by an innovative investment in information technology. For Allied Dunbar's sales function, it was a triumph.

But, only later was it discovered that it was not possible to relate this customer information to Allied Dunbar's corporate database. For about two years, the superb mine of information about customers' needs, wants, and aspirations, knowledge gained about competitors, and so forth, could not be exploited. It was either locked up inside the individual 3500 computers or else it was flushed out when there was no more space in the computer's storage.

Now, consider what would have happened if this opportunity to improve the process 'Offer products for sale' had resulted from a study such as that carried out by Doppler Electronics. Other owners of processes — like those defining new product requirements, developing new products, planning market strategies, and so on — would be much better served if they could have access to this constant, daily flow of real-world information. A model of the business, like that shown in Figure 11.4 (see page 129) would have revealed all of the strategically important information flows. The interface requirements for the laptop PCs would have been demanded and defined from the start and *all* would have benefited, without prejudicing the improvements in the 'Offer products for sale' process.

Allied Dunbar eventually bought the necessary hardware and software interfaces they needed to start capturing and storing this precious market information in order to benefit the business as a whole, but it was two years after the localized *functional* triumph of the salespeople. This represents a loss of two years of valuable data, and it cost financially, too — almost £950 000, probably *much* more than if the interface requirements had been defined at the start. This is *not* re-engineering.

The softly, softly approach — linked processes

Focusing on only one of the most critical business processes may or may not qualify as a re-engineering project. It does not matter. The point is to make the enterprise more competitive/effective. But, when the scope of the project extends to a number of linked business processes — and the linkages are all known, from the process-to-process model of the enterprise — then the re-engineering label will almost inevitably apply. The re-engineering label now has some significance, because of the orders of magnitude increases in resources and management attention needed to exploit the greater opportunity from a true re-engineering project.

For example, Doppler Electronics' list of most critical business processes included the following:

- Procure products
- Order products for warehouses
- Order products for stores.

These three processes are closely linked in providing the right goods at the right place so that customer needs can be profitably satisfied. All three of them were assessed to be quality D, bad. A glance at Figure 11.4 reveals all of their mutual dependencies for excellence, as well as their relationships with other critical processes. The entire management team at Doppler would be delighted if these three processes were moved from D, bad to A, excellent. And so would Doppler's customers.

This is a much bigger project than focusing on only one process. The organizational issues involved are much more profound. The technology and other resource requirements are larger. And the pay-off would be correspondingly bigger. An illustration of a linked process approach, and the impact it had on just one of the processes in the chain, comes from Ford in the United States. This example of re-engineering was described by Michael Hammer in his original *Harvard Business Review* article of July–August 1990.

Paying suppliers — immediately

Ford's process 'Pay suppliers' was slow and costly. At first sight, it is easy to say, 'The slower, the better!' About 500 people were employed in Ford's Accounts Payable Department. Taking a departmental approach, a study revealed that automating the process would show substantial savings by enabling a reduction from 500 to 400 people.

Then, a more holistic view was taken.

'Pay suppliers' was then seen to be only one of a linked set of business processes involved in getting the right components and raw materials at the right time. Rather than view 'Pay suppliers' from a departmental perspective, Ford viewed it from the perspective of the *set* of processes needed to do effective provisioning of components and materials.

The result was much more effective provisioning of the manufacturing plants. Within Ford's Accounts Payable Department, the result for the process 'Pay suppliers' was a reduction in headcount from 500 to 125, a substantially greater cost reduction than was foreseen from the departmental approach. Moreover, it resulted in very satisfied suppliers. Instead of waiting up to three months for payment, the cheque is sent automatically when the goods are received. (The excellence of supplier-visible processes is important in sustaining a good [= competitive] supplier-to-customer relationship for Just-In-Time deliveries of key components, which is exactly what Ford needs.)

The 'pay suppliers' process was improved in Ford as part of a re-engineering project of linked internal processes. Ford's truck division illustrates how this can be extended beyond the boundaries of the enterprise.

Win–Win with a single supplier

Ford's truck division has a *single supplier* of brakes. This means that the process 'Select suppliers' has to be truly excellent — imagine the consequences of failure — and the supplier-to-Ford interface processes must also be excellent. In Ford's case, they are.

Unlike the earlier example, Ford does not pay its supplier when a shipment of brakes is received; *it pays only when the brakes are used.* Ford's approach is, 'These brakes belong to you until we use them. Then they are ours, and we shall pay you immediately'.

> **At first sight, this may seem like bad news for the supplier, but not so. Ford has linked its manufacturing planning processes directly to its brake supplier by telecommunications. The supplier has the responsibility to manage its own manufacturing schedules and to manage Ford's inventories of brakes, but the supplier also has all of the necessary information to do this effectively. The reward for managing Ford's inventories of truck brakes is a lot of business for the supplier. Ford's reward is lower costs and highest quality. If the supplier optimizes Ford's inventory of brakes, they have to be zero defect brakes.**

This is a re-engineering project that goes beyond linking some of the enterprise's internal processes. It extends to a tight coupling with an external supplier's business processes. We shall see more examples like this.

Doppler Electronics' team decided on a softly, softly approach. Theirs was different to any of the options described up to now. It was not even a re-engineering approach, within the terms of the definition — that would come later.

The CEO decided to motivate each process owner (by means of an appropriate reward system geared to *process excellence*) to start improving each process towards its future desired state. Meanwhile, the information technology people were building the necessary telecommunications networks and providing the necessary measurement systems (described later, Chapter 19).

The enterprise's future desired state was sufficiently general to have relatively long-term validity, and so were the resulting process future desired states.

This is still softly, softly. Improving processes to the level of competitive excellence could be started while the infrastructure needed for more aggressive re-engineering of the business was being put in place. Each member of the top management team was actively involved in managing the improvement of at least one cross-functional process. Learning about managing cross-functional processes could take place within the existing structure of the organization, preparing the ground for more dramatic changes later. At a future time, they believed that the risks would be known and containable and the necessary basic infrastructure would be in place. A different team in the same enterprise might take a different view. That is their business, of course.

14

Quantum changes

Combining business processes

Doppler's study quite quickly revealed organizational and other issues involved in exploiting much more far-reaching re-engineering opportunities. This is where a really big pay-off can result from a dramatically different challenge to the status quo.

Consider again the following processes critical to the Total Competitiveness of Doppler Electronics:

- Procure products
- Order products for warehouses
- Order products for stores.

Why are they like that? Why do they have these particular and different executive owners?

Certainly, Doppler has taken a cross-functional business process approach — the technique used guarantees this — but the traditional functional *attitudes* have been preserved. Each of the three owners of these processes worked in each of three long–established, different business functions. It had always been like this. It seemed only natural that they should become the owners of these processes. And in Doppler's case, this was entirely correct, consistent with its carefully planned softly, softly approach.

Quite soon, however, people began to ask some penetrating question about these three processes. Why must they have different owners? What are they actually *for*? About a year after the study, when a lot of learning had already taken place, it was possible to think what was previously unthinkable, even to talk about it. Why not combine the three processes and define a single process called 'Provision stores'? This is what it is all about, really. The process would then have a single owner, as usual, and it would have its own competitively framed future desired state.

Now, the status quo can *really* be challenged.

A process called 'Order products for warehouses', for example, assumes a *need* for warehouses. As long as there is the process, there will be warehouses. A process called 'Provision stores' requires no such assumption. Maybe warehouses are *not* needed? After all, Federal Express and others are putting people out of the warehousing business. Alternatively, Federal Express can be viewed as taking over the logistics processes of its customers. Even some years ago, Federal Express began warehousing parts for IBM workstations. As a result, by using Federal Express aeroplanes and couriers, delivery costs were cut, and IBM was able to start closing 120 parts warehouses.

Maybe Doppler needs only *one* warehouse, and a small one at that? Maybe suppliers will deliver directly to the stores, maintaining stocks of their particular products on behalf of Doppler? Maybe? Maybe?

This is when the opportunities for business re-engineering really pay off. The climate has to be receptive, however. It could have been suggested a year earlier, at the end of the second day of Doppler's study, that these three processes could be combined to become 'Provision stores', and given a single owner. But it would have been rejected by this particular management team at that particular time. They needed to come to terms with the organizational and business process *learning*, to build the confidence needed to take the larger strategic step.

It has to be said that another management team in the same business might identify and embrace the bigger opportunity — and bigger risks — from the start. Again, *vive la différence!*

Combining processes for cost savings

BMW has combined its purchasing function with research and development and design. This is a functional combination, but the effect is to combine these processes under the ownership of one senior manager. For new model projects, the teams include designers, engineers, purchasing agents, and manufacturing people — that's quite cross-functional!

Four years before they start production, they know what a new car will cost, because the forward-purchasing agents have been in close contact with suppliers for two years before the design of a new model is 'frozen' — about four years before production starts.

BMW people can work on friendlier terms with its suppliers, which can deliver efficiency and quality benefits. For example, a sunroof, which was previously assembled by BMW from 60 different parts, now comes semi-assembled with only three parts, reducing the opportunity for error. BMW claims that this integrated approach is yielding cost reductions of at least 20 per cent, and up to 40 per cent in some cases.

Dispensing with business processes

We have seen how the historic roles of two or more processes may be challenged and then combined, in the interests of Total Competitiveness/Effectiveness. In fact, all processes should be challenged. Each one should be able to justify its continued existence in the enterprise or even to exist at all. The question to be answered is along the lines of, 'If we were to start the enterprise all over again next Monday, would we perform this process?' Today, perhaps, an outside supplier could do it better, and at a lower total cost to the enterprise. These were the questions that led the management of Laura Ashley to start paying Federal Express to perform all of the Laura Ashley logistics processes. In contrast, Benetton, while in the same line of business as Laura Ashley, at least in some respects, has taken a totally different view. It has invested heavily in a global set of logistics processes, tightly coupling the market-place — the cash registers in Benetton's shops — to its manufacturing plants in Italy, Spain, Scotland, and the United States. And Benetton does not just 'stick to the knitting', its traditional products. What it learns from the market-place has enabled it to build a $75 million business in such accessories as glasses, perfume, handbags, luggage and cosmetics. It is also developing a line of shoes, which Luciano Benetton says will be as important to sales as are its traditional clothing products.

It may have been traditional for an enterprise to do all of its personnel education and training in-house, but does it necessarily follow that this is the best way to perform the process 'educate and train personnel' today? You may be reluctant even to ask the question, but it must be asked. This process, and other former sacred cows, such as 'Manufacture products', 'Offer products for sale', 'Service installed products', and others, have all been 'out-sourced' by some enterprises, to their advantage. A typical example in the public sector is cleaning — from city streets to hospitals to nuclear power stations. And a business can grow from this. A European company such as Hoden International, with its headquarters in Holland, may start by taking on the cleaning processes, in a hospital in France, move on to doing the catering, then be asked to set up a retail outlet in the reception area, to the benefit of all. And we shall see how even external *customers* can do the work of 'Enter customers' orders' — British Steel, and many others — resulting simultaneously in lower costs and higher customer satisfaction. *This* is competitiveness.

There are other *groups* of processes that are being out-sourced today, in ways analogous to Laura Ashley's logistics group of processes. Many companies have dispensed with all of the processes concerned with providing and operating their information technology and telecommunications infrastructure, for example. Suppliers such as IBM, Electronic Data Systems (EDS), and others do it all, for a profitable fee, of course.

At the end of 1993, for example, EDS won the biggest outsourcing agreement ever awarded in Europe. This was for a ten–year £1 billion contract to run the computer systems for the Inland Revenue in the UK.

It is natural to respond, 'Of course, we must perform this process in–house!' when it has been this way for years, but try to reflect before giving a knee–jerk reaction. Think laterally. Think crazy. Just think. You can get good ideas at all levels of the business.

I contributed to a three-day conference attended by about 60 employees of North Sea Ferries. The participants were drawn from all over the company. There was the CEO and other Board members, ships' captains, catering people, accountants, clerical staff, pursers, cargo handlers.

The participants were divided into mixed groups, where they considered what were their individual activities. Then they were asked to describe what the activities would be like if they were competitively excellent — a sort of future desired state of the activities exercise. Some splendid ideas emerged, to the delight of senior management.

Like a number of other people, one lady was struggling to define exactly what she did. This is common. Many people find it easy to say that they, 'work in accounts' or 'in planning' but find it difficult to express what they actually *do*. Eventually, she decided that what she actually did was to negotiate insurance claims with commercial customers in the event of damage to their goods in transit.

It became even more difficult to define a state of competitive excellence for her activity (this is not easy, by the way). I suggested something like, 'All claims will be negotiated to the total satisfaction of the customer and North Sea Ferries'. I thought that was not bad, but it was met with silence and a furrowed brow. Then she said, 'To have the maximum competitive impact, the activity should not exist. There should be no damage. No damage; no claim. But that's impossible.' Immediately, three other members of her group leaned forward and started to speak. 'It could be done!', 'Suppose we ... ?', 'We could ... !', 'Why don't we ... ?' In no time at all, there was an animated discussion about all kinds of ways to make damage to a commercial customer's cargo virtually impossible. And these were people who knew their business. Some ideas seemed totally crazy. Never mind. The crazier the better. If you can think of it, someone else has probably already done it.

This is an example not so much of *dispensing* with a process, in the sense of paying someone else to do it, as totally *disposing* of it. There is nothing wrong with framing a process future desired state that says, 'In two years' time, this process will no longer exist'. One simple guideline is this: if a process or a subprocess or a task has no customers, no users of its outputs, then it has no reason to exist — it merely adds cost but no value. If in doubt, stop doing the process, then see how long it takes for anyone to notice.

These are not necessarily re-engineering opportunities, although some fairly radical re-engineering might be necessary in North Sea Ferries to effectively guarantee that there will be no damage to goods in transit. Letting an outside supplier perform one or more critical processes can hardly be described as re-engineering, either; this term should be reserved for what *you* do with your processes, not someone else. But, dispensing with or even disposing of processes may, nevertheless, represent real opportunities to improve Total Competitiveness/Effectiveness and these should be exploited, whether or not they can be classed as re-engineering.

Obviously you should not relinquish active ownership of what are sometimes called the 'core' processes of the enterprise. These are the processes the excellence of which will really differentiate it from competitors. Benetton views its logistics processes this way. Coloplast, making its colostomy bags, would regard it as insane to allow the process 'Manufacture products' to be performed outside of Denmark, let alone out-sourcing it to someone else. The company's particular, unique skills in designing and developing the manufacturing processes are a key source of its competitive advantage, and so should be retained at all costs (for an excellent discussion of this topic, see 'The Core Competences of the Corporation', by Prahalad and Hamel, *Harvard Business Review*, May–June 1990, and 'Competing on Capabilities: The New Rules of Corporate Strategy', by Stalk, Evans, and Shulman, *Harvard Business Review*, March–April 1992).

Optimising the enterprise

One valuable outcome from Doppler Electronics' study was the process-to-process model of the business that was produced (see Figure 11.4, page 129). This is just another way of illustrating the information contained in Figure 11.2 (see page 124), the internal supplier-to-process-to-customer matrix. And that matrix is simply a way of displaying the answers to Question 6, 'Who are the suppliers of necessary inputs?', for internal suppliers.

Earlier, it was said that this model could be greatly simplified. Any such simplification would be welcome — there are 60 'S's on the matrix shown in Figure 11.2. Each 'S' represents an *essential* supplier-to-process relationship, that something has to flow from one to the other, otherwise the future desired state of a most critical business process is at risk. But each 'S' also represents an opportunity for yet more meetings, negotiations, travel, additional costs, lost time, measurements, administration, and general hassle. So, any reduction, *without prejudice to the owners of the processes needs*, is important. The technique that can be used to do this is easier to do than to describe, but, like all of these things, it is based on a very simple chain of thought, as follows:

- Mr Brown is one of my suppliers
- Mr Green is another of my suppliers
- Mr Green is also a supplier *to Mr Brown*
- Mr Brown and I have a common supplier in Mr Green
- Mr Brown's essential inputs from Mr Green might include what *I* want from Mr Green
- in this case, I may chose to get my inputs from Mr Green *via Mr Brown*. Then I retain Mr Brown as a supplier and drop Mr Green.

And I know exactly what I want from Mr Green, and I know exactly what Mr Brown wants from him. This was revealed in the answers to Question 5, 'What are the inputs needed by each critical process?' I also know what I want from Mr Brown. I simply add what I require from Mr Green to my list when I negotiate with Brown. I have removed some redundancy, but I still get all that I need.

This is the simplest case. In another situation, Mr Brown may be negotiating most of my needs (for his own process), but not all. I then have to consider Mr Brown's process and decide whether or not it would be reasonable to include my *additional* requirements from Mr Green when I negotiate with Mr Brown. If this can be done successfully, I drop Mr Green as a supplier. Mr Brown is doing some additional negotiation with Mr Green on my behalf.

Doppler Electronics' matrix (see Figure 14.1) shows how it is done in practice.

Somebody has to start. And it makes a difference. As soon as I remove Mr Green from my list of suppliers, he may become unavailable as a common supplier to another pair of business processes.

One way to go about this is to start with the process that has the largest number of suppliers and, therefore, is possibly the most in need of help. In Doppler's case, this was 'Monitor personnel motivation', with all ten of the other processes identified as key suppliers. The owner of this process rejected all opportunities to reduce the number of suppliers by this means. The owner's view was vehemently expressed along the lines of, 'My process is category E. It never existed before in Doppler. When I look at its future desired state, there is only one way I can get what I need, and that is face-to-face with each of you!'.

Next, was 'Merchandize products', with seven internal suppliers. The owner studied the supplier-to-process-to-customer matrix and looked for common suppliers, in the same way described earlier for Mr Brown and Mr Green.

Figure 14.1 shows an extract from Doppler's matrix. The first 'S' at the top of the column belonging to the 'Merchandize products' process identifies 'Define market strategies' as a key supplier. When we search for *common* suppliers to both

159

Define market strategies	P				S
Procure products	S				S
Order products for warehouses					
Order products for stores					
Merchandize products	S				P
Monitor the competition	S				S
Monitor product quality					S
Monitor customer complaints	S				S
Review technology opportunities	S				S
Identify/cultivate key opinion formers	S				
Monitor personnel motivation					S

Figure 14.1 Extract from Doppler Electronics' internal supplier-to-process-to-customer matrix showing suppliers common to the 'Merchandize products' and 'Define market strategies' processes

'Merchandize products' and 'Define market strategies', the process 'Procure products' is revealed. Further down, we see 'Monitor the competition' is also a common supplier, as well as 'Monitor customer complaints' and 'Review technology opportunities'. There are no others.

The owner of the 'Merchandize Products' process now considers what would be flowing between the common suppliers and the process 'Define market strategies'. If

'Define market strategies' will be collecting most or all of what 'Merchandize Products' would need from, say, 'Procure products', then 'Procure products' may be removed as a supplier to 'Merchandize products'. The essential inputs will flow *to* 'Merchandize products' *from* 'Procure products', but *via* 'Define market strategies'.

Notice that the process owner must have the final say in deciding whether or not to take the option of removing a supplier process. Despite another process being a potential source of all that is needed from the common supplier process, the owner of 'Merchandize products' has to be able to say, 'That's as may be, but this is so important to me, I intend to negotiate and monitor my inputs directly, with no intermediary'.

When this is done for all seven of the key supplier processes for 'Merchandize products' (page 124), *all* of the common supplier opportunities are revealed to the owner. They are shown below.

Process:	**MERCHANDIZE PRODUCTS**
Supplier process:	**Define market strategies**
Common suppliers:	**Procure products**
	Monitor the competition
	Monitor customer complaints
	Review technology opportunities
Supplier process:	**Procure products**
Common suppliers:	**Define market strategies**
	Monitor the competition
	Monitor product quality
	Monitor customer complaints
Supplier process:	**Monitor the competition**
Common suppliers:	**Define market strategies**
	Procure products
	Monitor customer complaints
	Monitor personnel motivation
Supplier process:	**Monitor product quality**

161

Common suppliers:	**Procure products**
	Monitor the competition
	Monitor customer complaints
	Review technology opportunities
	Monitor personnel motivation
Supplier process:	**Monitor customer complaints**
Common suppliers:	**Monitor the competition**
	Review technology opportunities
Supplier process:	**Review technology opportunities**
Common suppliers:	**Define market strategies**
	Procure products
	Monitor the competition
	Monitor customer complaints
Supplier process:	**Monitor personnel motivation**
Common suppliers:	**Define market strategies**
	Procure products
	Monitor the competition
	Monitor product quality
	Monitor customer complaints
	Review technology opportunities

The owner of the 'Merchandize products' process can now consider the options, based on what will flow between the processes listed, and decide whether or not a supplier could be removed without prejudicing the essential inputs. Two suppliers were removed: 'Monitor product quality' and 'Monitor customer complaints'. The owner decided that the essential inputs from the 'Monitor product quality' process could be obtained from the owner of 'Procure products'. Inputs needed from 'Monitor customer complaints' would be negotiated with the owner of 'Monitor the competition'. The number of suppliers to 'Merchandize products' was thereby reduced from seven to five.

Next, it was the turn of the owners of the processes of 'Define market strategies', 'Order products for stores', and 'Monitor the competition', each of whom had six key suppliers. And so on.

The easiest way to handle this in practice is with a fairly simple program run on a personal computer. The owners of each process can then be presented with the full range of common supplier options, rather than having to search among the 'S's on the matrix. The computer also keeps the matrix current by only displaying the remaining suppliers, as some are removed during the process. It can also display the essential inputs identified for each process-to-process relationship, to assist in making the decision whether or not to remove a supplier. For enterprises that already use 'Groupware' or 'Teamware' (a linked set of personal computers and appropriate special software to run meetings, planning sessions, and so on), this is an ideal application.

Figure 14.2 shows the end result for Doppler Electronics after quite a cautious approach to removing suppliers. A zero indicates where a supplier has been removed from the vertical column belonging to a process. So, for 'Merchandize products', there is a zero for 'Monitor product quality' and 'Monitor customer complaints'. They were removed as suppliers to 'Merchandize products' in the way described earlier. Despite Doppler's management team's rather cautious approach, there are 15 zeros on the matrix. The number of 'S's has been reduced from 60 to 45, without prejudicing the needs of the owners of the processes — a worthwhile reduction (and 10 of the remaining 45 'S's belong to 'Monitor personnel motivation').

The optimized matrix may reveal additional opportunities for re-engineering. Notice that the owner of 'Monitor customer complaints' has lost six *customers*, retaining only three of the original nine. Losing six customers means that the owners of six processes, with a critical need for inputs from 'Monitor customer complaints', have decided that they can have their needs met via another process. Which one? When the individual decisions of the owners of these six processes are analysed, it turns out to be 'Monitor the competition' that has been viewed as the intermediary for the inputs from 'Monitor customer complaints'.

Define market strategies	P	S			S	S			S	S	S
Procure products	O	P	S	O	S	O	S		S		S
Order products for warehouses			P	S							S
Order products for stores			S	P							S
Merchandize products	S			S	P	S		S			S
Monitor the competition	S	S		S	S	P	O	S	S	S	S
Monitor product quality		S		S	O		P				S
Monitor customer complaints	O	O		O	O	S	S	P	O	O	S
Review technology opportunities	S				S		S	S	P	S	S
Identify/cultivate key opinion formers	S	O				O			O	P	S
Monitor personnel motivation					S	S	S			O	P

Figure 14.2 Doppler Electronics' internal supplier-to-process-to-customer matrix optimized

Now, perhaps, we have another opportunity to challenge the status quo. Earlier, we were able to consider replacing three processes with one: 'Provision stores'. Now, we might also consider combining — with very good reason — 'Monitor customer complaints' and 'Monitor the competition' into a single process called, for example, 'Monitor the marketplace', with a suitably framed future desired state and a single owner, and give it appropriate resources, of course. All of the needs of the customers of the newly defined process are known — they are those that exist for the process 'Monitor the competition', plus any additional needs of the remaining three direct customers of 'Monitor customer complaints'. This might qualify as a re-engineering project with regard to the '... fundamental re-thinking; radical re-design of business processes; to achieve dramatic improvements ... ' part of the definition.

If we assume that Doppler decides to create the combined process 'Provision stores' and also combines 'Monitor the competition' and 'Monitor customer complaints' into something like 'Monitor the market-place', the resulting internal supplier-to-process-to-customer matrix is that shown in Figure 14.3.

This is a lot simpler than the original matrix of Figure 11.2 (see page 124), but the organizational implications are profound. Combining these five processes to make only two — 'Provision stores' and 'Monitor the market-place' — will be hard work, but with a worthwhile pay-off. The longer the chain of coupled processes, the harder it is to re-engineer or transform, but it is exactly this that makes it very difficult for a competitor to replicate.

There are now only 8 most critical business processes, instead of 11, and there are only 33 'S's instead of 60 (7 of which still belong to 'Monitor personnel motivation' — the owner resolutely rejected the idea of reducing this number), yet nothing has been lost.

Restructuring the process

You will recall that a generic future desired state for an enterprise has been used for Doppler Electronics — to maximize its Total Competitiveness — as the vehicle for illustrating the main points of the technique described in this book. Now imagine that it is a little over a year since this first study was done and Doppler's top-management team answered the seven key questions. The team's members have learned a lot since that first meeting. They have met

Define market strategies	P	S	S	S		S	S	S	
Provision stores		P	S		S	S		S	
Merchandize products	S	S	P	S				S	
Monitor the market-place	S	S	S	P	S	S	S	S	
Monitor product quality		S			P			S	
Review technology opportunities	S		S		S	P	S	S	
Identify/cultivate key opinion formers	S						P	S	
Monitor personnel motivation			S	S	S			P	

Figure 14.3 Doppler Electronics' internal supplier-to-process-to-customer matrix for re-engineering

again to review the enterprise's future desired state and to see if any changes to the rest of the analysis are necessary.

Doppler's team modified its future desired state at this meeting. One small phrase was added to the original one, so it now says:

> **We shall maximize the total Competitiveness of Doppler Electronics in a pan-European context.**

They decided to exploit the opportunities of the Single European Market by acquiring appropriate, established companies in other centres in the European Community. Adding these four words to the enterprise's future desired state makes a big difference. All of the previous answers to the other six key questions must now be evaluated against this new future desired state (as well as any other changes that have taken place during the previous year, independent of this self-imposed change).

It is not likely, in view of the change to the future desired state, that Doppler's team will arrive at exactly the same 11 most critical business processes. Purely for illustrative purposes, however, and to keep it simple, let us assume that this is indeed the case.

Next, they decide to reduce the number of processes to eight, as described earlier, by creating two, new, combined processes: 'Provision stores' and 'Monitor the market-place'. When we move on to consider Question 7 again, 'What is the most competitive structure of each critical process?', the answers will be different, in the pan–European context.

There are those two sub–questions again:

1 'Where will each process be performed?'

2 'If in more than one place, what level of coupling is appropriate between the different locations?'

Of course, there are all kinds of management issues to be resolved when moving from a UK perspective to one that is pan–European — personnel, linguistic, cultural, accounting, legal, and so forth. These are beyond the scope of this book, but the internal structure of the most critical business processes (at least) must be decided, otherwise the whole thing will not work properly, and this internal structure *is* within the scope of this book.

The new future desired state for the enterprise tells us that Doppler's team are not simply buying other companies' assets and cash flows. They have defined their job as being to maximize the Total Competitiveness of the whole pan–European enterprise. So, the internal structure of each process must be such that it enables it to contribute as much as it can to the Total Competitiveness of the enterprise.

Nobody can do it except the top–management team — they own the processes.

It helps to start with a clear knowledge of the way things are done today; where is each process performed and what is the current level of coupling within each process?

Figure 14.4a shows the structure of Doppler's eight most critical business processes as they are today, a company operating solely in the UK.

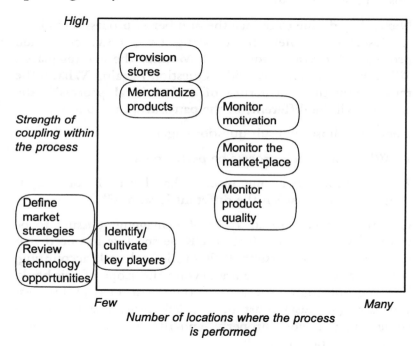

Figure 14.4a The structure of Doppler Electronics' most critical business processes when solely a UK operation

Figure 14.4b shows the internal structure of these process that, the management team has decided, would be most effective to maximize the competitiveness of their business in a pan–European context.

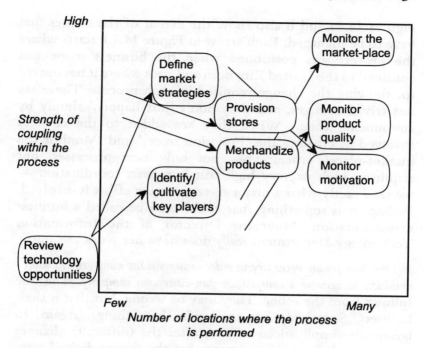

High

Strength of
coupling
within the
process

Few

Many

Number of locations where the process
is performed

Figure 14.4b The most effective structure of these processes for pan-
European operation of the company

The only process that remains unchanged is 'Review
technology opportunities'. 'Define market strategies' is now
performed in every country where Doppler is present, rather
than centrally, but with very strong internal coordination.
There is also very strong coordination within the process
'Monitor the market-place', though it is now done in every
location. 'Identify/cultivate key opinion formers', is no longer
performed only in the UK. The CEO still owns the process,
and he performs it in the UK, but he took the view that the
French General Manager was probably better equipped to
perform this process in France, the German General Manager
in Germany, and so on. Nevertheless, there is an appreciable
level of coordination within this process, for good business
reasons. And so on for the other processes.

Figures 14.4a and b also show the extent of the *changes* that have to be managed. Each arrow in Figure 14.4.b starts where the process was positioned when the business scope was confined to the United Kingdom and ends where it has moved to, showing the change required in each process. These are not trivial changes, and they don't 'just happen' simply by announcing them. When they are added to the changes involved in creating the 'Provision stores' and 'Monitor the market-place' processes — not only new processes, but requiring high or very high pan-European coordination — we see exactly what a major re-engineering effort is involved. Perhaps it is something that could even be called a business transformation. Now the Director of the Information Technology Department *really* does have her work cut out!

Yet the changes are necessary in order to support the management team's ambition to become a competitive pan-European company. The one follows from the other. They may be wrong, but that is their business. Somebody has to decide these things. Again, to ignore the implications of this, after the (difficult) changes have been defined, is to accept that the future desired state will *not* be accomplished. It could even be a factor in deciding to change the future desired state again, to remain only a UK company. But, what then?

Try this for your own enterprise, even roughly. Position your key business processes on the diagram, as Doppler's team did, the way they are today. This should be easy. You really ought to know where each key business process is performed and what is its current level of internal coupling.

The next step is more difficult. Where should each process be positioned on the diagram in order to make the maximum contribution to Total Competitiveness/Effectiveness? It may well be difficult, but it has to be done. Otherwise, if there are desirable or necessary changes, and they are not recognized and implemented, your Total Competitiveness/Effectiveness is not what it could be. The changes may be very large — even enormous, qualifying as re-engineering projects, according to the definition — or they may be quite small — quick and simple to implement. Either way, *not* to implement them is to reject the opportunity. Again, that is your business.

15

Extending the enterprise

Opportunities with suppliers

The Ford example shows how excellent supplier-to-enterprise processes can improve competitiveness, from the perspective of the external customer. The result should be lower costs and inputs of a higher quality, leading to greater pricing flexibility and products of a higher quality. Ford wins; its customers win. This win–win situation should be the ultimate yardstick for judging an upstream opportunity regarding suppliers. After all, it is at the *customer* interface where Total Competitiveness/Effectiveness is evaluated. But the supplier also should win, of course.

Doppler's key external suppliers for its most critical business processes have all been identified. This was done in the process of answering Question 6, 'Who are the suppliers of necessary inputs?' Until now, the focus has been on the *internal* supplier-to-process-to-customer relationships. In most cases, these are where the biggest opportunities will be found. Now, though, we should add the external suppliers to the process-to-process model of the business. The result is shown in Figure 15.1.

The external suppliers are known process by process. That is how the question was answered. In Figure 15.1 they have been consolidated. For example, three owners of processes might have identified consumer electronics product manufacturers as a key supplier, for identical or for totally different inputs. Six owners might equally well have indicated market research organizations as a key supplier.

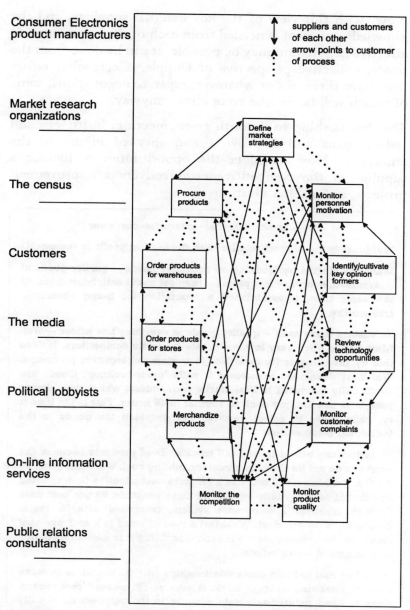

Consumer Electronics product manufacturers

Market research organizations

The census

Customers

The media

Political lobbyists

On-line information services

Public relations consultants

suppliers and customers of each other

arrow points to customer of process

Define market strategies

Procure products

Monitor personnel motivation

Order products for warehouses

Identify/cultivate key opinion formers

Order products for stores

Review technology opportunities

Merchandize products

Monitor customer complaints

Monitor the competition

Monitor product quality

Figure 15.1 Doppler Electronics' process-to-process business model, including external suppliers

173

Now, with this view of the key external suppliers, and the knowledge of what is needed from each of them, much more effective negotiation may be possible. It can be done from the single, collective perspective of Doppler Electronics, rather than have three, six or whatever, separate negotiations, some of which will be for the same inputs anyway.

This has nothing to do with re–engineering, but it can still reduce costs and improve the quality of inputs to the enterprise. Now, consider the opportunities to include a supplier in the competitiveness/effectiveness improvement projects, as Ford has illustrated.

Win–win–win: supplier–enterprise–customer

Wal-Mart is the biggest retailer with the highest profit in the world.

Wal-Mart started by focusing on customer needs — quality goods at guaranteed, everyday low prices — then set about satisfying them. At the same time, it established a reputation for being absolutely trustworthy.

To sustain these ends — quality goods at everyday low prices — Wal-Mart has to have very low costs, relative to its competitors. It does this by investing in its invisible (to customers) logistics processes. Wal-Mart developed a concept it calls 'cross-docking'. Goods are continually delivered to Wal-Mart's warehouses, where they simply pass from one loading dock to another in 48 hours. This is the time it typically takes to select, repack, and despatch the goods to the individual retail outlets.

Wal-Mart can afford to buy full truckloads of products because the products do not lie about in inventory, adding cost. Wal-Mart owns its trucks. Running a full truck is a lot more cost-effective than running one that is only partially loaded. Of these products, 85 per cent pass through Wal-Mart's warehouse system, compared with its major competitor's 50 per cent. Wal-Mart's cost of sales is 2 to 3 per cent less than the average for the industry, enabling it to sustain its policy of guaranteed lower prices.

Wal-Mart had to build close relationships with its suppliers to make the cross-docking concept work. It uses satellite-based communications to send point-of-sale data directly to its suppliers on a daily basis. This means that some suppliers, such as Proctor and Gamble, can automatically replenish stocks of their products on Wal-Mart's

---

shelves. (In contrast, its main competitor frequently changed suppliers in a constant effort to shave a little more off the price.)

Wal-Mart has created a tightly coupled set of business processes, using information technology, which reaches out to the customers and back to its suppliers. It is very fast and responsive, has lower relative costs, and is extremely difficult to replicate. It has not invested in technology to get rid of people, but, rather, its success has enabled it not only to be the biggest and highest profit retailer in the world, it added more jobs than any other US company in 1993. By contrast, Sears Roebuck and Company shed 169 000 people in the same year, according to *Business Week*.

Early in 1993, the consulting firm Kurt Salmon Associates released a study which concluded that US grocers could cut their costs — and impact prices — by 11 per cent, or more than $30 billion a year by establishing paperless links with their suppliers. This would mean more effective merchandize assortments and store promotions and eventually to a continuous replenishment of shelves based on what is sold each day. An excellent, re-engineered 'provision stores' process at Doppler Electronics might look like this.

Opportunities with customers

Using a little imagination will show you how to extend the linkage of internal business processes out to external *customers*. Again, you should explore all avenues to do this, to create a happy liaison with customers, to the total dissatisfaction of your competitors. British Steel shows how this can be done.

Selling scrap — at a premium price

British Steel gave terminals to some of its customers, enabling the buyers to look directly at British Steel's unallocated stock file, and place orders directly. The 'unallocated stock' results from making too much steel in a normal production run. This is common.

It is profoundly embarrassing to make only 950 tons, say, for an order of 1000 tons. The cost per ton to make the final 50 tons could be very high — or you can buy it from a competitor, then sell it on. So, you make a bit extra and the excess tends to lie about and eventually rust.

> **Then it gets scrapped.**
>
> **British Steel was able to promise very fast delivery because the steel was in stock. So it charged a premium price. Customers got what they wanted, and British Steel made a direct contribution to profits of about £6 million per year. Both parties won.**

This is not re-engineering, but it is a nice way to improve the customer-visible process 'Offer products for sale', *and* get the customer to do the work of order entry. Notice that this example is also quite easy to copy. The next example is different. It shows how mutually competing suppliers can work together with the process 'Offer products for sale', to the satisfaction of each competing company *and* to their customers.

> **HMV UK is a typical customer of the record manufacturers. It has about 185 shops in the United Kingdom, selling records, videos, and so on. Like the other record shops, its major profit opportunity comes from pop music items, which have a life of only three or four weeks. HMV is in the fashion business, and most of its fashion products are bought on Saturdays.**
>
> **If HMV cannot get sufficient stock of the hot items for Saturdays, it loses out on its peak opportunities. Previously, it was a costly and not very effective nightmare ordering from the competing major record manufacturers. HMV places 60 per cent of its orders on a Monday. In its Oxford Street store in London, nine bored and frustrated employees used to spend hours dialling, queuing, and redialling the various record suppliers, often failing to secure what was wanted.**
>
> **Then, three major UK record manufacturers – EMI, BMG, and Polygram – worked together with a software house to provide a solution. Even though the three of them are mutually competitive, they have a common interest in getting their hot products to the record shops. They *also* suffered from the Monday morning bottleneck.**
>
> **Now, they offer a 24-hour, 7-days-a-week service to record shops. The system is called EROS. Each shop using EROS is provided with a personal computer containing a catalogue of over 40 000 items, representing the currently available product range of EMI, BMG, and Polygram.**
>
> **EROS users create their orders on the personal computer, validating them against the current catalogue. The catalogue is updated automatically every week, with up to 1000 changes and additions.**

> **The stores not only know _what_ is available, they know the _format_ of the item — vinyl, cassette, CD, video, special collections, and so forth.**
>
> **EROS now serves over 700 shops, including more than 200 independent outlets. With only three manufacturers involved, it does not cover all of the field, but they represent up to 60 per cent of the industry. For HMV's Oxford Street store, for example, it means that four people, not nine, can get the orders in on Monday, and be sure that the products (from these three suppliers, at least) will be available the following Saturday.**

Despite being mutual competitors, this is a win for the three record manufacturers, for their customers, the 700–odd record shops, and for the consumers, too.

Opportunities with alliance partners

Until now, we have considered only the internal opportunities and those involving external suppliers to foster the win–win situation at the customer interface, in other words, to foster Total Competitiveness/Effectiveness. But, there is another community of people, different to suppliers, that can improve this win–win with customers — strategic alliance partners. Strategic alliances are becoming increasingly common. Indeed, the Vice-President of Corporate Development at Olivetti has said that the 1990s will not so much be characterized by competition between individual companies as by new, complex corporate groupings.

The distinction between a strategic alliance partner, a customer, and a supplier is simple. While the customer pays the seller and the seller pays the supplier, the strategic alliance relationship does not depend on the exchange of money for goods and services. It is established for another reason — access to a market, technology, particular skills, and so on.

> **Motorola has an alliance with Toshiba; Motorola gains access to the Japanese market; Toshiba gains access to Motorola's technology. ICL, the UK computer company, has a similar alliance with Fujitsu. Daimler's AEG opened a $2 billion microelectronics joint venture with Deutsche Aerospace with the objective '... to keep an iron grip on the intelligent part of a car'.**

Both parties to the alliance must have a win–win situation if the alliance is to be a good one. This means excellence of the 'partner-visible' business processes at the interface between them. But, the real reason for the alliance should not be forgotten, which is, namely, to improve Total Competitiveness/Effectiveness. There is no point in investing in a wonderful win–win with an alliance partner if it does not enhance the, commercially, most important interface — that with the customer.

Like the seller–customer relationship, negotiations with a strategic alliance partner often take place at a very senior level. The day-to-day working of the alliance will usually be at a more operational level. This is analogous with the potentially disastrous 'Bill customers' or 'Deliver products' process situations described earlier. Without the right controls, all kinds of valuable, proprietary information can leak from one partner to the other, far beyond the initially negotiated limits.

> Fujitsu manages the partner-visible processes very well. Its many alliance partners can only gain access to Fujitsu through a single gateway, which is rather euphemistically called 'The Collaboration Section'. This is where Fujitsu can monitor and control access to its critical information, skills, technologies, and so forth. It is also where careful questions can be asked of any alliance partner who appears at the gateway — questions regarding customers, competitors or markets, for example — the answers to which can be analysed and distributed to appropriate places throughout Fujitsu.

Often nowadays, the alliance relationship is sustained by telecommunications. Boeing is connected by a high-speed link across the Pacific to its two Japanese partners for on-line development of the new Boeing 777. If the right controls are not in place, the potential for high-speed leakage between enthusiastic design engineers can easily be imagined.

Of course, an alliance partner can simultaneously be a customer and a supplier as well.

Texas Instruments is a customer of IBM UK. It is also a key supplier, linked to IBM's procurement processes via Electronic Data Interchange (EDI), in other words, computer-to-computer communication. Texas Instruments is also an alliance partner of IBM UK, for the development and marketing of computer-integrated manufacturing systems.

In the simplest case, the customer has no interest in the supplier-visible or partner-visible processes. Both kinds are invisible to the customer, such as the seller's 'Pay suppliers' process. But when the customer is *also* a supplier, and even more so when they are an alliance partner as well, much more of the seller's business is revealed. Otherwise invisible processes have *become* customer-visible. This exposure can be dangerous if some of the supplier-visible and/or partner-visible processes are bad.

In this simplest case, the customer does not really care if the seller has a terrible 'Pay suppliers' process, if they only part with the money they owe after 90 days of mutual recrimination. The bad smell quickly becomes more obvious when the supplier is *also* a customer, however.

On the other hand, if all these visible processes are excellent, it fosters even more strongly the win–win at the commercially most important interface — the one with customers. The US pharmaceutical products distributor McKesson illustrates how an opportunity with alliance partners can be exploited. McKesson did not start improving competitiveness by focusing on alliance partners. That came later.

Pharmacists tend to have little or no loyalty to their suppliers. They just want fastest possible delivery, to help them to keep stock levels down. McKesson gave hand-held terminals to the pharmacists, who were then able to place orders directly on to McKesson's computer systems. The pharmacists can also enter their profit margins. The terminal can then print their own price labels. Because the pharmacists placed their orders directly, this enabled McKesson to provide a guaranteed, fast delivery service.

> **95 per cent of the pharmacies in the US are now on-line to McKesson and able to enter their orders this way. They win; McKesson wins.**
>
> **McKesson does not manufacture anything. It took only a little imagination, and a lot of money, to go on-line to McKesson's over 2000 suppliers. This enabled McKesson to reduce the number of people employed in its Purchasing Department from 140 to 13. Over 50 per cent of McKesson's own purchase orders are automatic, computer-to-computer.**

McKesson had established a highly responsive, very expensive, but highly profitable, set of linked business processes to capture and retain customer loyalty. It had effectively re-engineered its business, which is merchandising. Then, someone had a bright idea, saw a new opportunity.

> **Most of the pharmaceutical products sold in the US are subject to an insurance claim. McKesson went on-line to the major health insurance providers — a set of alliances, sustained by telecommunications — and offered to process insurance claims for a 5 per cent commission. McKesson is now performing the process, 'Process insurance claims'. This process is far beyond the set of business processes traditionally associated with someone in the merchandising industry. McKesson does it so well, though, that it has become the largest third-party processor of such claims in the United States. A totally new, profitable revenue stream has been created, to the satisfaction of the consumers (the customers of the pharmacists) and of its health insurance alliance partners.**

This goes beyond re-engineering. You can only really *re-*engineer something that is already there. In McKesson's case, what was there was the business of merchandising pharmaceutical products. McKesson needed two things to move on to the next stage, to what some people are calling 'business transformation', or 'business redefinition'. Again, the label is less important than the act. First, McKesson needed the platform — the information technology and telecommunications infrastructure, the attitudes and expertise, and so on — resulting from its re-engineering efforts (which were done *before* the term was invented). The second essential was someone with the bright idea.

This second factor — someone with a bright idea — is a crucial element in *all* of the examples quoted in this part of the book, 'Selecting the opportunities for competitiveness'. Ultimately, it is the creativity of *people* that produces such winning ideas and makes them work. There is no substitute. Answering the seven key questions merely reveals the raw materials from which to identify and select the opportunities. It just happens to be a very complete and effective way of doing it. The numerous examples from the real world quoted here (and there are many more in the Appendix at the back of this book) can then serve to stimulate the imagination and convince people that it *can* be done. But, after that, it is up to you.

16

The continuum of opportunities

To summarize, carrying out a study of your enterprise as set out in this book will reveal a continuum of opportunities to improve its Total Competitiveness/Effectiveness, which ranges from simple, quick-to-implement projects, through re-engineering of a single process, or a group of processes, right through to a total transformation of the enterprise through re-engineering. Whatever you decide will be the first project, the ultimate objective should be acknowledged by all, which is to implement in full the implications of the study (as modified by subsequent returns to the enterprise's future desired state and its Critical Success Factors, of course). Not to acknowledge this is to accept that the enterprise will remain less competitive/effective than the boss and the top management team have decided that it should be.

So, even if a softly, softly approach is adopted, such as that taken by Doppler — and there is nothing wrong with this — with no projects initially that could be described as re-engineering, the team should be encouraged to identify the more challenging projects that will inevitably become necessary if it is to achieve its future desired state.

Figure 16.1 is a useful way in which to structure this kind of thinking regarding possible projects. The vertical axis gives a rough measure of the time it is anticipated it will take to exploit the opportunity; it could be equated to the scope and complexity of the project. The horizontal axis relates to the size of the challenge the project poses to the status quo. This

	Small status quo change	Large status quo change
Long term	Do differently	Re-engineer
Short term	Fast pay-off	Pilots

Figure 16.1   Matrix to assist thinking about projects to maximize opportunities for competitiveness

can be equated to what is sometimes called the size of 'the paradigm shift'.

Re-engineering projects

By definition, business re-engineering projects belong in the top right-hand square of the matrix shown in Figure 16.1 — fundamental rethinking, radical redesign, and so on. And there is a continuum of positions within this 'Re-engineer' square. Re-engineering one business process might be located in the lower left-hand corner of it, for example, while transforming the entire enterprise would tend to be in the upper right-hand part of the square. Building the First Direct bank would fit into this square, as would the examples from Federal Express, McKesson, and Ford described earlier.

The upper right-hand corner is for enterprises that have 'reinvented' themselves — where the changes are so dramatic, the enterprise emerges as a different entity. John F. Welch is doing this to the giant General Electric Company, creating what he calls 'the seamless corporation' out of what was a plodding, bureaucracy-laden behemoth. Motorola has gone through a number of transformations — from car radios, to television, to mobile telephones and pagers (it is the global leader in this last area).

Boeing is apparently starting to move from being engineering- and technology-driven, with jealously guarded boundaries between functions and divisions. Now, there is a much stronger focus on cooperation and team working across the old boundaries. Its President of the commercial plane group has said that the focus now is on cutting cycle times, reducing inventory, and improving processes (sounds familiar?): 'We are convinced that 35 to 40 per cent of everything we do is non-value-adding'.

British Airways is another company that has so radically changed itself that it could almost be called a reinvention (I remember the 'doggy bag' days in the 1970s, when they gave you a plastic bag with plastic food and plastic cutlery as you entered the plane; after that, you were on your own). SABENA, on the other hand, is an example of an airline that still has a long way to go.

Most senior management teams are reluctant to 'bet the business' and initiate this level of transformation, even when it is recognized as being necessary. The chaos, conflict, and upheaval involved are deemed to be just too much to handle. Nevertheless, at a meeting of the Inter-Company Productivity Group in Arundel in England, late in 1993, some senior executives were saying '. . . we want more powerful treatment, even if it is painful'.

Pilot projects

On the other hand, re-engineering just one business process might be sufficiently short term, yet be a significant enough challenge to the status quo to be called a pilot project, and so be located in the lower right-hand square. It should be remembered, however, that a pilot project should be regarded as the first step, the means for learning how to migrate from the 'Pilots' square to the 'Re-engineering' square.

McKesson did not start its costly service to 95% of pharmacies in the US all at once. A low-cost, low-risk pilot project with, say, half a dozen good, friendly customers would do, just to see whether or not it would work and to iron out any human and technology problems, for example. Even so, this is quite a radical departure from the status quo. Apart from anything else, McKesson has changed part of the business process 'Process customer orders' from being invisible, to being customer-visible, *and the customer is happily doing the work*! Indeed, there were so happy to do it that, quite soon, they were ordering from McKesson in preference to McKesson's competitors.

Then they began to complain if McKesson did not have a particular product in its range. This enabled McKesson to expand its product range, not in response to some inspired guesses in the marketing department, but in response to known customer demands.

Notice how this has grown from being a small, pilot project to one that embraces the entire supplier-to-customer chain of business processes, with McKesson in the middle. McKesson has created a dynamically self-balancing system to the delight of its customers and suppliers, and with massive benefits to McKesson. Formerly, 800 sales representatives sold $915 million of products. By the late 1980s, 375 of them were selling $3 billion. The company came from nowhere to become fourth in *Fortune* magazine's list of the most admired companies in its sector.

Now this really *is* business re-engineering. In fact, it is closer to business transformation. McKesson's core business was originally in dairies and dairy products. The pharmaceutical distribution business was a small offshoot that was being considered for sale in the late 1970s. Today, however, McKesson has had to sell its *core* businesses to pay for the information technology and telecommunications needed to sustain its very successful distribution business. Notice that it is quite easy to copy the idea of giving a few terminals to customers — unless a competitor has already got there first — but it is massively difficult to replicate the customer-orientated money machine that McKesson has created. Being difficult to copy is another desirable characteristic of re-engineering.

Fast pay-off projects

The lower left-hand square is where to position opportunities for competitiveness that do not come within the scope of the definition of re-engineering, but which, nevertheless, deliver a significant competitive benefit, quickly. There is no radical challenge to the status quo. It could be as simple as staggering the lunchbreak so that there is always a real person to answer customer telephone queries instead of a telephone answering machine playing Vivaldi's 'The Four Seasons', yet again.

The owners of processes should constantly be looking for such opportunities. They tend not to cost very much and they can deliver significant benefits quickly. If the process owner cannot think of anything, you can be sure that the people lower down in the hierarchy *will* be able to.

Retaining customers pays dividends

The CEO of MBNA America, the credit card company, led a company-wide drive to see why customers left. Naturally enough, it provided valuable lessons on how to keep them.

Each department had to find which single factor (maybe two) had the biggest impact on retaining customers. Daily measurements of these factors, and an appropriate reward system for improving them, had a dramatic impact. After eight years, MBNA America's industry ranking went from 38th to 4th. Profits were multiplied 16 times in that period.

Notice that this did not result from a dramatic re-engineering of the business. Nor did it arise from a study such as that carried out by Doppler Electronics. It was simply a case of asking the right questions of the right people and focusing on the people who pay their salaries — the customers. MBNA's financial results show that it makes sense. Evidence from the United States and the United Kingdom indicates that it costs only about a fifth as much money to retain existing customers as it does to acquire new ones.

It is very important that the opportunities in the 'Fast pay-off' square be taken and done excellently. They may need levels of commitment from senior management similar to those needed for a re-engineering project.

The management team of one of my clients was asked to identify potential opportunities and then position them in the matrix shown in Figure 16.1. Having been told about General Electric's approach to the process 'Monitor customer complaints', there was unanimous agreement to install and announce a similar '800' telephone service to encourage customers to communicate with the company. They positioned this in the 'Fast pay-off' square: 'We could get it installed within a week! ', was the cry — quick installation, quick impact, quick benefit.

When I asked, 'Who is going to answer the phone?' the room became very quiet.

The team suddenly remembered that General Electric's system only works properly because the people answering the telephones are extremely well trained and are supported by technology that enables them to answer almost any query, *to the total satisfaction of the caller.* When the telephone is answered by someone who says, 'Sorry, I don't know — I'm just a temp', it is worse than having no reply at all. It reveals a contemptuous management attitude to calls from the outside.

Just as for the other three, the 'Fast pay-off' square represents a continuum of opportunities. At the bottom left-hand corner are things that can be implemented and deliver a benefit next week. At the top right-hand corner of this square are projects that will take longer to implement and which are bordering on being re-engineering projects. And a small project in the lower part of the 'Fast pay-off' square can migrate upwards and to the right. Bausch and Lomb, the contact lens manufacturer, shows how a more substantial investment can have a big impact on resolving the universal telephone problem.

Bausch and Lomb uses a relatively new telecommunications service called Integrated Services Digital Network (ISDN) to attack this problem. ISDN enables the caller's number to be identified, automatically. If a caller hangs up, even quickly, the number is passed to the first available Bausch and Lomb representative, who calls back immediately. Customers are astounded (and delighted) that Bausch and Lomb take this trouble.

This is not re-engineering, and it is easy to replicate, but a little imaginative thinking would show how the facility could be extended so as to result in even greater competitive impact and customer satisfaction. American Express has done this. When a customer calls American Express, the system automatically routes the call to the right person. While the service representative is picking up the telephone, the customer's latest account status is presented on the representative's computer screen. An informed dialogue can begin, straight away.

'Do differently' projects

The upper left-hand square is for projects that do not represent such a radical challenge to the status quo that they can be classed as re-engineering, but which may be large and expensive. Beware starting such projects today. Instead, ask yourself whether a more radical approach — a re-engineering approach — might deliver quantum levels of improvement. Usually, the act of going through the work of answering the seven key questions together will open up people's minds, expand their imaginations, and stimulate lateral thinking far beyond the historically imposed mental limits that were in place before the study began.

188

All the same, sometimes a competitive opportunity will remain positioned in the 'Do differently' square for all of the best possible reasons. The fact that it is not a re-engineering project should make absolutely no difference. It is a valid competitive opportunity, to be exploited like any other.

Thinking about projects

At the end of the study, it is useful to have the management team spend some time thinking about the four quadrants of Figure 16.1 in the light of what has been revealed during the process of answering the seven key questions. The team's members should be asked to identify specific projects, aimed at their most critical business processes and their future desired states, and position them in the four quadrants. They should feel uneasy if there are no 'Fast pay-off' projects. If there is nothing in the 'Pilots' or 'Re-engineer' squares, they will be guilty of complacency, arrogance or a total lack of imagination. Any large projects that preserve the status quo, being placed in the 'Do differently' square, should pass the test of close scrutiny and questioning to see whether a more valuable re-engineering opportunity can be created.

For projects that really *are* re-engineering projects, some work done by three consultants with McKinsey and Company's New York office indicates that big pay-offs, in terms of '... dramatic improvements in critical, contemporary measures of performance ...' are associated with projects that pose a really big challenge to the status quo (see 'How To Make Re-engineering Really Work', by Hall, Rosenthal, and Wade, *Harvard Business Review*, November–December 1993). They identify two major components in such challenges to the status quo. One is what I have called 'scope'. So, 're-engineering' a subprocess or task that lies entirely within a department of one function is small scope. Re-engineering the combined process 'Provision stores', however, would be a large-scope project for Doppler Electronics.

189

The other component of the challenge to the status quo they call 'the depth of the business change'. This means, to what extent the re-engineering will challenge the following:

- roles and responsibilities
- measurements and incentives
- organization structure
- information technology
- shared values (that is, the 'culture' of the enterprise)
- skills.

A glance at the above factors makes it clear that something which is such a big challenge to the status quo will probably be a disaster if there is no strong leadership from top management. Hall, Rosenthal, and Wade suggest that the CEO should, typically, be involved some 20 per cent of the time at the beginning, growing to 50 per cent. Moreover, the winners saw implementation not as a once-and-for-all effort, but as a series of waves washing over the enterprise for a period of years, leaving a system in place for continuous improvement (this issue of continuous improvement will be addressed later, in Chapter 20).

Part 5

EXPLOITING THE OPPORTUNITIES FOR COMPETITIVENESS

Introduction

The main theme of this book is how to find the re-engineering and other opportunities to become more competitive. The techniques described up to now should enable most top-management teams to get started in challenging their status quo, at least, and find their unique opportunities. They *are* unique. No two management teams are the same. No two enterprises are the same. There is a number of other issues that must be addressed by the top management team if the benefits are to be realized in practice, however. Some of them are discussed in this final section on exploiting the opportunities for competitiveness.

This section is not about the details of implementation as this is beyond my knowledge. There are many other works and sources of expertise on the successful definition and management of large and small projects. Rather, it discusses some strategic issues that must be addressed, including information technology and telecommunications, issues regarding the structure of the organization, defining the appropriate measurement systems, and so forth. There are many other issues to be resolved, of course. Here, I shall be discussing a subset of them.

The word 'competitiveness' is, again, deliberately used in preference to re-engineering, for the same reason as in the previous section. We have seen that some very worthwhile competitive opportunities will *not* be re-engineering opportunities, by definition, because of their scope and/or the size of the challenge to the status quo. And we have seen that there is another category, illustrated by the McKesson's 'Process insurance claims' example. This is not strictly *re-*

engineering because the process did not previously exist in McKesson, but it was, nevertheless, a competitive opportunity to be exploited. By the way, beware of people who speak disdainfully about something that is not classed as re-engineering. Lots of excellent opportunities can be missed by taking this attitude. A Swedish colleague has told me, for example, that there are consultants in Sweden who have embraced re-engineering with a messianic fervour that he describes as being almost akin to religious fundamentalism: 'If it is not re-engineering, it is a heresy!' Such people are not confined to Sweden.

We begin with information technology and telecommunications. For the sake of brevity, these will be lumped together as 'information technology', unless there needs to be specific reference to their separate roles.

17

Information technology

There may be all kinds of wonderful technologies a hundred years from now, but today's 'enabling technology' for virtually all re-engineering and other competitive opportunities is information technology. It is essential that the top management team understand the nature of the beast, so to speak. The trouble is that many of today's top managers entered the workforce about the same time as the enterprise's first computer, and their paths have never crossed subsequently.

Sir John Harvey-Jones, former chairman of the UK chemical giant, ICI, put it in his splendidly direct manner at a networking exhibition in the UK in June 1993. He said, 'Top managements are generally not computer literate and don't realize that information technology makes it possible to devise different ways of running a business. An awful lot of boards are still run by old people who have not grown up with IT, so they fail to see how a dynamic interactive organization can be built up, both inside the company and with suppliers and customers. This makes change extremely difficult. The biggest problem remains a lack of vision at the top. Over the years we have always had very hierarchical organizations, with very little delegation of anything. To get the real payoff from IT, you have to totally change your business, rather than just mechanize the operation.'

Particularly for re-engineering and business transformation projects, the sheer size of the cost of the technology component takes on a commercial dignity of its own. And the technology is such an integral (and integrating) part of the project that top management *must* be involved in setting the strategic agenda for information technology. Times have changed from the days when a CEO once said to me, 'I have a chap who looks after these things'. These technologies have become too important to be left to the technicians.

It is taking a very long time for this message to get through, however. A *'Computerworld'* survey of *Fortune 1,000* CEOs revealed that 64 per cent doubted the value of their investments in information technology. Whose fault is it? I suggest it is *their* fault for letting such an expensive and potentially strategic resource get out of control.

Another study in the US showed that 82 per cent of information services executives were feeling pressure to quantify the value of spending on information technology. They are the wrong people to ask! The only people who can say whether or not it is of value are the users. If information technology is acknowledged to be playing an essential role in increasing Total Competitiveness/Effectiveness, there can be no doubting its value. The job of the technicians is to provide the right technical infrastructure at a competitive cost performance, just like any other support service.

We can use McKesson to develop a model of a re-engineered enterprise, to illustrate the inextricable role of information technology in the company's success.

Remember that McKesson started by capturing and retaining customer loyalty through hand-held terminals, on-line to McKesson's mainframe computers. The technology provided the means for a happy marriage between seller and buyer, to the growing discomfort of McKesson's competitors.

This is illustrated conceptually by the model at the top of Figure 17.1. There is an actual physical overlap between McKesson's business and that of its pharmacist customers, sustained by the technology that created the win–win situation. We can imagine all of McKesson's customer-visible business processes lying within this overlap.

McKesson's management knew why they had made this

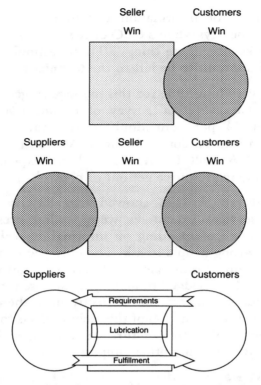

Figure 17.1   Models of McKesson's re-engineered enterprise and the role of information technology in its success

investment in information technology — *it was to gain market share*. They knew how to measure its success.

Going on-line to its external suppliers fostered the happy marriage between McKesson and the pharmaceutical and other product manufacturers. They have been added to the middle of Figure 17.1. Again, there is an organizational overlap, which is where McKesson's supplier-visible processes will be found.

McKesson's management team know why they made this investment in information technology, too — *it was to drive cost out of the business*. Having acquired customer loyalty, let's keep it *and* make some profit. So they knew how to measure it.

All McKesson has done is to couple the widely dispersed pharmacies (with the need) to the widely dispersed manufacturers (with the products) via a linked set of its own business processes.

The bottom of Figure 17.1 illustrates the sets of processes involved, and the role of information technology in this. There is a set of linked business processes that starts in the market-place and goes through McKesson and out to its suppliers. We can call them the 'Requirements' processes. They have to be fast and efficient. McKesson has made them fast and efficient, as we have seen.

There is another set of linked business processes that starts within the suppliers and finishes within the pharmacies, McKesson's customers. We can call them the 'Fulfillment' set of business processes. These *also* have to be fast and efficient, or else costs go up and customer satisfaction goes down.

In the middle is another, different set of business processes, which I call the 'Lubrication' processes. These are neither in the 'Requirements' set, nor in the 'Fulfillment' set, but they are just as important. It is here that we find the processes of hiring, education and training of personnel, management development, legal, financial and building services, security, information services, and so on. Their purpose is to provide the right quality and quantity of 'lubricant' at the right time and place — money, skills, advice, premises, information, and so on — to the 'Requirements' and 'Fulfillment' processes, and to each other. If they do not provide the right lubricant or there is not enough of it or it is too late, one of the processes will begin to slow down, to squeak, or fail altogether. Up go costs again and down goes customer satisfaction.

Before carrying out a study like that done by Doppler Electronics, it is not possible to say whether the major opportunities for any enterprise are in the 'Requirements', 'Fulfillment' or 'Lubrication' processes or in some combination of all three. There are always surprises. But, you can be quite certain that the whole thing will have a crucial dependence on information technology. Many examples have been given already of enterprises that have become more competitive (many more are given in the Appendix at the back of this book). All of them rely on information technology as the enabling technology. The best of them have used the technology in ways that enable different processes of the enterprise to be coupled together, and then out to customers, suppliers and/or strategic alliance partners. Such was the case with McKesson.

These chains are getting longer. DuPont makes fibres. It is on line to a customer, Milliken, which makes fabrics. Milliken is on line to one of its customers, Leslie Fay, which makes garments. In turn, Leslie Fay is on line to Dillard's Department stores, where the garments are sold. This is a long chain of linked business processes, but with very fast reaction to changes in tastes in the market-place. Four totally independent enterprises are coupled together to their mutual benefit, and, hopefully, to the benefit of the people wanting to buy the garments.

This requires a holistic view of business networking *and* the technology requirements which goes far beyond anything discussed up to now.

The bottom part of Figure 17.1 shows, at least conceptually, what a fully re-engineered enterprise looks like. All the process–to–process connections are in place to support the necessary information flows, *between* the processes. All the internal connections are in place, *within* each process, to support its competitive internal structure.

All the opportunities to connect directly to suppliers and customers are in place to support other competitive opportunities. (Strategic alliance partners and the alliance-to-enterprise connections can also be added to this model, of course.)

But Doppler Electronics' top-management team has already created a detailed version of this model, simply by answering the seven key questions (see Figure 15.1, page 173). This is their 'business network', the strategic requirement statement that effectively defines their need for information technology. And there is clearly a lot more detail embedded in the answers to the seven questions than is shown in the model. The technicians can now get on with defining the technology strategy, holistically. No more incompatible islands of automation. No more dead-end projects. Moreover, the management team has the means to *measure* the effectiveness of their investment in information technology — how well does it support the owners of the business processes collectively and individually in maximizing Total Competitiveness? Information technology has to provide the necessary infrastructure to support the 'Requirements', 'Fulfillment', and 'Lubrication' processes, and their connections within and beyond the enterprise. Telecommunications provides the pathways, within and between the processes and beyond the enterprise. Computer applications, databases, and so forth, are *within* the processes. Doppler's management may have chosen a softly, softly approach, but they all understood the nature of the journey they were about to undertake.

The bottom part of Figure 17.1 is not simply a model of McKesson's enterprise or even a model of the pharmaceutical merchandizing business; it is a schematic representation of almost any enterprise — a bank, an insurance company, a government department, a supermarket chain, a foundry, an avionics manufacturer, an airline.

There is an acronym, CIM, which means computer integrated manufacturing. This linking of business processes started in some manufacturing companies to support Just-In-Time delivery systems for materials and components.

Figure 17.1 would work as a model of a company that has fully implemented CIM. Change the meaning to computer integrated *management*, and Figure 17.1 still works. It becomes valid for *any* enterprise. It describes a management approach, *and* the technology, that drives costs out of the enterprise, improves quality, reduces cycle times, and increases customer satisfaction — the purpose of re-engineering and all those other good things.

But an excellent information technology infrastructure — and a computer-literate management and workforce — provides much more than this alone. It enables new, unpredictable things to happen inside people's brains, anywhere in the enterprise. To quote Professor Freeman Dyson, a theoretical physicist, 'The great task before all of us is to organize our societies in such a way that unpredictable things have a chance to happen'. Change the word 'societies' to 'enterprises' and we can relate this to information technology.

British banks first organized their computer systems by customer account number. That was how transactions were recorded. Now, they want to reorganize their systems to work by customer name, like First Direct, to enable them to offer more sophisticated services and initiate more effective, targeted marketing. One bank in the UK has estimated that such a change would cost about £1 billion and take about five years. This is much too long, but it has to be done. The enterprise with a properly instituted infrastructure to support computer integrated management has its adaptability built in, so to speak. First Direct has the infrastructure, the management, and the attitudes to make massive shifts, quickly, when the technology and consumer environment presents an opportunity to do so.

> **British Airways has this kind of infrastructure, sometimes called 'the information technology platform'. Such built-in flexibility is illustrated by the way it has taken hotel business away from competitors. People normally make their flight reservations *before* they book hotel rooms. Quickly, and at little extra cost, British Airways added the facility to its service to book hotel rooms at the same time as the traveller reserves the flights. This took a lot of business away from some hotel chains, to British Airways' associated hotels.**

The AMR Corporation, parent of American Airlines, tried a

similar hook-up with Marriott, Hilton Hotels, and Budget Rent A Car. This was a huge computer project and a huge disaster; a $165 million write-off in 1992, and even bigger sums involved in legal damages claims.

Computer applications are about as predictable as anything can be made to be. It is how they are made; computers do not get bright ideas. But, give people access to information, and we can foster such creativity. Machines are not very good at inventing new questions. This uniquely human facility becomes much better if the answers are easier to access. Then, even better questions become even more valuable. Providing Doppler's management team with the infrastructure shown on Figure 15.1 (see page 173) is just the beginning, the predictable piece. Switch it on, then watch the sparks fly!

Within a year of their study, Doppler's information services people had provided each process owner with the kind of information support needed to stimulate creative thinking.

Each member of the top management team has a touch-sensitive personal computer. Turn it on, and Doppler's future desired state appears on the screen — the real one, not the generic version used in this book. This is a constant reminder of what the team is supposed to be doing with the assets of the company. Touch the screen, and Doppler's eight Critical Success Factors appear.

Against each Critical Success Factor is a traffic light, coloured red, orange or green. Green means that progress towards achieving this Critical Success Factor is on target — in other words, the processes whose excellence is necessary for its achievement are being performed according to plan. Orange means that one or more processes have drifted off plan and so the Critical Success Factor is being compromised. Red means that there is a big problem with one or more of the necessary processes for that Critical Success Factor.

Imagine a Critical Success Factor that is showing red or orange. Touch this screen at this Critical Success Factor and the complete list of processes that need to be performed to a standard of competitive excellence in order to achieve it are displayed. These are taken directly from the Critical Success Factor/process matrix shown in Figure 7.3 (see page 80) Against each of these *processes* is a traffic light — red, orange or green, corresponding to the status of a problem, giving a warning, or saying things are all right, respectively.

Touch the screen for any of these processes and it fills with the name of the process, the name of its owner, the process future desired state, and the five measurements the process owner has accepted as the basis for monitoring the process. And, again, against each measurement is a traffic light, showing its status as red, orange or green.

Now the process owner (or any other member of the top-management team; the system is transparent to all of them) can get into the detail of any measurement that has an orange or red light, for example. There is a direct connection between this executive process owner's information system and the operational systems of the company, as it is directly coupled to the cash registers in its stores. Statistical analysis tools, historical searches, product-by-product comparisons, store-by-store comparisons, trend information, customer perceptions, competitor information, and so on, are all available, plus the means to model and display the results. The owners of the processes not only have the dials in front of them, they have the levers of control, too.

To summarize, the senior people in the company have decided what is important and what they are going to achieve in measurable terms. The systems have been built to provide information on the current status of each measure, compared with its target. Achievement or otherwise is starkly shown and is visible to all senior executives — no more long, often unintelligible, reports that are late anyway; no more hiding data until someone else can be found to blame. Moreover, this is not a report that appears at intervals. It is an ever-present reminder to senior management of their objectives, targets, achievements, and shortfalls. It does not just provide information. It also acts like the manager's conscience, sitting on their desks and reminding them of the fundamentals of the business. It is this that sets it apart from many other systems; the fact that it is integrated into the heart of the management process. The system is constantly growing and improving in its ability to stimulate unpredictable innovation. This is beyond re-engineering.

Doppler's process-to-process model, including its customers and suppliers (see Figure 15.1, see page 173) represents a huge amount of change — re-engineering, at least. Most of the very large information technology investments will be needed simply to stitch it all together and make it work. There will not be many degrees of freedom in the strategy regarding technology necessary to provide the appropriate infrastructure. For example, any retail bank today will have automatic teller machines (ATMs) to dispense cash to customers who use a plastic card and enter a PIN (personal identification number). Clearly the technology used in these machines must be decided and dictated from the centre. You cannot allow a local bank manager the freedom to select the supplier.

Even at an international level, there has to be coordination, even between different banks. In Spain, for example, I can simply insert my UK Lloyds Bank Access card (Mastercard) into a Spanish ATM and it gives me Spanish pesetas. But, if the local manager of that Spanish bank does not have access to the tools and information needed to make *that branch* more competitive, all it is is mere technology. The innovative factor, one of those unpredictable bright ideas that are uniquely human, which are important for that manager's particular part of Spain, these are what the information technology must also support.

The next thing that Doppler's team must do is to cascade access to this precious mine of information and analytical tools down and across the rest of the company. After all, they have a Critical Success Factor (Number 6) which says, 'We

203

must enable/empower our people to perform to their full potential'. These are powerful *enabling* tools. It is said that information is power. Once this access to information is cascaded down, *empowerment* follows automatically. You cannot stop it, except by withdrawing access to the information. And empowerment always flows down.

This will require large expenditure on information technology. There will be seismic changes of an organizational and personnel nature. All of it is a necessary consequence of following the thread from the future desired state of the enterprise to this point. It would make absolutely no sense to ignore the implications of this work, done by the most senior people in the enterprise. Management teams who believe that they cannot or will not accept the implications of these large changes should not do the study. It will be too frustrating.

18

Issues concerning organizations

Some of the material in this chapter is drawn from *'How to Manage Managers'* (McGraw-Hill, 1994), which I co-authored.

The changing structures of organizations

Most of us have spent our working lives in highly structured, hierarchical organizations. It was not always like that. The typical nineteenth-century enterprise was more like that shown at the top of Figure 18.1. Pretty well all the knowledge and information were concentrated in the thin top layer.

The 'command and control' structure (lower left of Figure 18.1) evolved from the armed services, particularly after the Second World War. It served well in the post-war growth years, when simply to be in business was usually enough to make money. The demand and growth provided lots of opportunities to move up the management ladder — and to add more rungs. Even today, some enterprises have as many as 20 levels or more between the CEO and the entrance-level employee.

The management triangle lower right of Figure 18.1 is another way of representing this structure. The number of people employed at any level decreases as you move up the triangle.

Things started changing in the 1960s and 1970s with the introduction of computers. They automated many of the

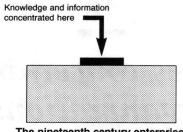

The nineteenth century enterprise

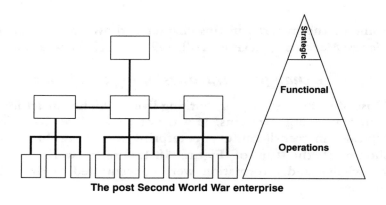

The post Second World War enterprise

Figure 18.1 The changing structures of organizations

transaction processing jobs, such as payroll, general ledger, accounts payable, maintaining stock records, and so forth. The management triangle changed to something like that shown at the top of Figure 18.2.

The top piece of the triangle remained about the same size. The number of people on an average board of directors was more or less constant between 1960 and 1980. It may have become just slightly larger because of new directors being appointed for new functions such as Personnel, Finance, Information Services, and so forth.

At the bottom, though, the relative numbers *decreased* dramatically as a result of computer-based transaction processing.

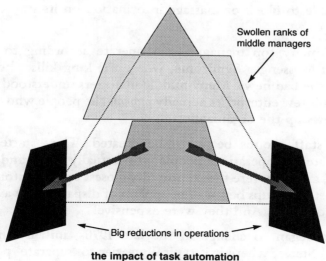

Swollen ranks of
middle managers

Big reductions in operations

the impact of task automation

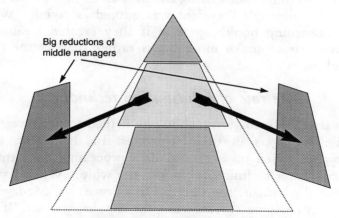

Big reductions of
middle managers

the impact of decision support systems

Figure 18.2   The changing enterprise

The other change was that the bit in the middle grew. This bit is where we find the middle managers. In many companies their jobs changed. Formerly, middle managers translated the strategic decisions from the top into revenue–generating actions. Later, as their numbers and layers grew, they tended to become mere collectors and filters of information. They

207

were able to block or massage information on its way up to the top.

Sadly, many top managers still operate according to The Persian Messenger Syndrome, where the king kills whoever brings the bad news. Many middle managers understood this. After all, few enterprises actually *promote* the people who carry bad news up the organization.

Large staff groups began to be created. They started to dominate the operations people who actually made and sold things, and *they* were the community closest to the customers. These staff groups began to be spoken of disparagingly as 'the bean counters'. And they were expensive!

Things began to change in the late 1970s, initially in the United States, where it is typically easier to 'separate' people (what used to be called firing them) than in Europe. In 1983, one US company's President was quoted as saying. 'We've been rewarding bookkeepers as if they created wealth ... business has to make more beans rather than count them several times'.

The role of information technology

For a time, information technology helped to preserve some middle managers in their fortresses. In the 1970s, most enterprises relied on a central data processing department. The computer technicians cracked the whip. (When I was a computer salesman, the Group Data Processing Manager of one of my customers warned me, the day that we met, 'If ever you talk to any of my users, the next machine will be bought from your competitor. I know better than the users what their needs are'.)

Then, mini–computers became available. By and large, they were forbidden by the computer people, of course. Soon, a mini–computer came to be defined as, 'Any computer that can be hidden in a middle manager's budget'. You could very quickly count up 15 different office machines that were individually programmable, needed their own group of experts, and for which the word 'computer' never featured on the invoice.

It was a way to get around the tyranny of the computer people and their two–and–a–half–year backlog of work. It was also a way around the central site's high standards of hardware selection, software, security, standards of operating hygiene, data management, programming, documentation, and so on.

Quite soon — to the despair of the mainframe computer people in their enterprise data centres — incompatible islands of automation sprang up all over the place. Each one was sufficiently unique to preserve the boundaries of the mini-empire that it served.

But not for long.

If you look at the bottom of Figure 18.2, you will see what happened. This change was driven by computer departments evolving from being mere processors of data — transaction processing — to being providers of information. The personal computer began to proliferate in the early 1980s and brought added impetus to this change. And personal computers were cheap enough that, if the enterprise would not pay for one, ambitious managers would buy their own. In complete contrast to the nineteenth-century situation, information and knowledge came to be spread throughout the enterprise.

There were still massive incompatibilities between the different computer systems. In most enterprises, they continue to exist today. But, quite quickly, some people who actually took decisions could have the necessary information before their eyes — on time, unfiltered, unpolluted — and they had the power to evaluate alternatives at their fingertips. Those who simply made recommendations became redundant.

Some of the information does not even pass before the eyes of real people nowadays. We have seen how computers handle it directly in the case of McKesson, for example.

The McKesson situation is highly structured. In the new organizations, information and networking will be all-pervasive. When professionals and managers throughout an organization can communicate with each other this way, horizontal links between peers in different locations — and beyond the enterprise — become established, regardless of any formal organization structure. Yet, such links are important for people to lend a hand to each other or provide some information, a practical tip. Consider Doppler's process-to-process model again.

Once, it was thought that information technology would depersonalize enterprises. Now, though, we see it binding scattered employees into an integrated whole. And the good enterprises make sure that their people can gain access to it, to stimulate those unpredictable, bright, crazy new ideas that are so vital to the enterprise's success.

In a growing number of enterprises, these horizontal ties between people are replacing the old vertical ties as *the* means of activity and communication, *even where the old vertical structures are still formally in place.*

Unfortunately, many of these numerous enterprises that have gone through the pain of downsizing and delayering to arrive at the rather strange-looking structure shown bottom of Figure 18.2, despite the layoffs, still have the same basic command and control structure as before. Even after all the cutting that has taken place, too many layers of management still retard decision making and lead to unnecessarily high coordination costs and excessive response times.

The future winners will be those enterprises that manage to migrate to the cross-functional business process view exemplified by McKesson (see Figure 18.3). It is more logical, in competitive terms. It is the organizational response to the need to achieve shorter cycle times, faster time to market, lower total costs, coming closer to Total Quality, and higher levels of customer satisfaction. And all this means gaining ground towards the goal of Total Competitiveness/ Effectiveness.

210

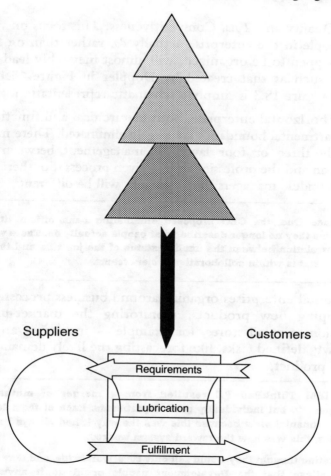

Figure 18.3 The model towards which today's slimmer enterprises should be moving

The horizontal enterprise

Some people are calling such a structure 'the horizontal enterprise' (there is an excellent article on it in *Business Week* 20 December 1993). Whatever the label, it is a natural consequence of challenging the old pyramidal structures, with all of their functional boundary wars that get in the way of

Total Quality and *Total* Competitiveness. This focus on what the people in the enterprise actually *do*, rather than on how they happen to be organized, will almost inevitably lead to a model such as that created by Doppler in Figure 15.1, of which Figure 18.3 is simply a schematic representation.

In the horizontal enterprise, both hierarchical and functional or departmental boundaries are largely eliminated. There might be only three or four layers of management between the chairman and the professionals in a given process. So, there will still be middle managers, but their jobs will be different.

> **At Banc One, the CEO proposed eliminating bank officer titles because they no longer describe what people actually do. There was no correlation between the implied status of the job title and their actual status within collaborative project teams.**

Horizontal enterprises organize around business processes — developing new products, monitoring the market-place, provisioning retail stores, for example — instead of around narrowly defined tasks, like forecasting the likely demand for a new product.

> **The IBM ThinkPad PC resulted from a merger of mutually antagonistic but individually good departments. Each of them took a departmental view because this was the way it had always been. Besides, this was how the reward system worked.**
>
> **Marketing thought they would sell only 6000, worldwide, and they did not believe that the Development people could do it anyway. Development *knew* they could do it, but they had no confidence that Marketing would be able to sell the product, and they were equally convinced that Manufacturing would not be able to build it.**
>
> **At last, someone at a sufficiently senior level must have realized that the old, contentious way was no good. A team was created that focused on the product, rather than on individual departmental excellence. The boundary wars were extinguished. The ThinkPad 700C came out in three months. The market-place liked the product, particularly the screen and the keyboard, and the price performance was competitive.**
>
> **Not *6000*, but *100 000* ThinkPads were sold, in the first 53 days.**

In the US, other companies moving in the direction of the horizontal enterprise include American Telephone and Telegraph (AT&T), DuPont, General Electric, Xerox, and Motorola. Lexmark International is another, an independent company that was formerly a division of IBM and which makes and markets printers, and similar products. Of its managers in manufacturing and support, 60 per cent have gone since it became independent, in favour of global, cross-functional teams.

AT&T's Network Systems Division identified 13 'core' business processes. Its approach is to give each core process an owner and a 'champion'. The owners focus on the day-to-day operations of their process, while the champions ensure that the process remains linked to overall business strategies and goals. Collaboration is key.

New enterprises, such as Midland Bank's First Direct, have an easier task. There are no organizational barriers in existence. Another example is Astra/Merck Group. This is a new company formed to market anti-ulcer and anti-high blood pressure drugs, licensed from the Swedish drug company, Astra. Astra/Merck is structured around six 'market-driven' business processes, from drug development to product sourcing and distribution. Its director of strategic planning has commented that a functional organizational structure, '. . . wasn't likely to support our strategic goals to be lean, fast, and focused on the customer'. This means competitive.

The *Business Week* article mentioned at the start of this section quotes consultants in this field reporting that '. . . companies are rushing to organize around processes without linking them to their key goals!' This is management fad and fashion madness. Doppler Electronics may one day become a horizontal company, but the thread that will lead to this becoming a possibility originates within Doppler's future desired state. More probably, as few organizations will choose to be either *totally* vertical or *totally* horizontal, Doppler will be a hybrid, like the majority. The management team's softly, softly approach may appear cautious, but it has left all of its options open.

19

Measuring critical business processes

Most people accept the truth of 'if you can't measure it, you can't manage it'. Yet, even when a measurement is apparently critical to the enterprise, people simply do not do it. Is it too demeaning? Too threatening?

An example from a survey of the European transportation industry carried out by consultant Stephen Byrne for GE Information Services in 1989 makes the point. People were moving over to Just-In-Time delivery systems; deliveries *must* arrive on schedule. However, only 54 per cent of shippers claimed to measure reliability of the transport services they use and only 33 per cent could quote statistics of reliability even though reliability was often quoted as being a key issue and a prime criterion in the selection of carriers.

Like the shippers, the carriers regarded reliability as of primary importance and an essential selling point of their services, yet 75 per cent of the sample simply failed to measure their performance in this area in any way.

Critical business processes have to be *managed* to a state of competitive excellence. They don't just get there by themselves. So, appropriate measurements are essential.

The key word here is 'appropriate'. For example, Doppler's future desired state for the 'Monitor customer complaints' process is all about making it easy for customers to communicate with the company, *and* transmitting the complaint to the most appropriate manager. The owner of the process is not rewarded for *reducing* the number of complaints. Indeed, if the raw measurement of the number of complaints is decreasing, this might indicate a failure of the process owner to make it easy for customers to communicate with Doppler. They may simply have given up trying.

The best-qualified person to define the measurements is the process owner. At this juncture, owners' eyes tend to glaze over and they look worried. 'How on earth can you measure something like "Identify/cultivate relationships with key opinion formers" or "Define market strategies"?', they exclaim. It may be difficult, but it has to be done. Otherwise, you may have an out-of-control process, and nobody knows until it is too late.

In fact, it is not as difficult as it seems. The owners of the processes now have a lot of information, a lot of sources of inspiration for defining their key measurements. Here are some of them.

1 *The process future desired state* This is the ultimate one, particularly if the executive reward system is changed (as it should be) to reward excellence of the owner's *process* rather than excellence of the owner's *functional* entity, such as finance or marketing, for example. If half of your earnings next year will be geared to progress in closing the delta between where your process is today and its future desired state, you will find a way to measure it. If not, your spouse will!

2 *Satisfying customer needs* For internal customers, the process owner now knows what their needs are, the outputs from the process that are the critically needed inputs to *their* processes. Either you or your internal customers (or both) measure your performance against the negotiated criteria. Why both? Surely, in a team-working environment like this, it is sufficient for just *one* of the internal owners to do the measuring? Why not the supplier process, or the customer process? Naturally, this has to be based on accuracy, honesty, and trust. But why not? The cost saving could be worthwhile.

If yours is a customer-visible process, you have to go out and negotiate with the *real* customers. This does not mean your opposite number on the customer's Board of Directors. It means the people who actually use or depend on the outputs of your process. Think about the 'Bill customers' process in this light for a moment. You will find that the real customers will be delighted to help you to define appropriate measurements.

3 *Suppliers* For internal suppliers, if it has been agreed that only the owners of the internal *supplier* processes will do the measuring, then, as an internal *customer*, you do not need to do any measuring. But you still have to negotiate your needs for inputs. For *external* suppliers, you have to negotiate your needs, either directly or via a colleague, another owner of a process. Negotiating the need effectively describes the measurement. Depending on your relationship with the external supplier, you may or may not wish to perform your own, independent monitoring of the supplier's performance.

4 *Within the process* Here are three elements worthy of consideration.

- *The level of employee satisfaction* You can have the most superbly planned process in the world, with wonderful technology, and so on, but if the people working in it do not want to play your particular game, it will fail. (In Doppler's case, the owners of each process could make their requirements known to the owner of 'Monitor personnel motivation'.)
- *Efficiency* Effectiveness is doing the right things — improving towards the process future desired state and satisfying the needs of internal and external customers (if any). Efficiency looks *inside* the process boundary. Are the process resources being properly used? Is there any unnecessary work, repetition, avoidable time delays, and so forth. In other words, how wisely is the money being spent inside the process?

- *Adaptability to change* This, also, is inside the process. How long does it take to change a customer's name and address on file so that the next invoice or delivery goes to the right place? A day, a month, six months? You don't know? Adaptability to change is a key factor in maintaining a process at the level of competitive excellence. Throw a change at it and see what happens. Measure it. The owners of the processes should be constantly on the look-out for any means to improve process adaptability.

A process owner can repeat the seven key questions study with the *process* management team, which the process owner has to create. The process future desired state is known. The team then identifies the Critical Success Factors, the most critical subprocesses or activities, and so on. Just as before, all of the subprocesses *must* be within the defined scope of the process. They are owned by the process owner. Getting down to, and answering Question 7. 'What is the most competitive structure of each critical *sub*process?' might provide opportunities to optimize the process, and reveal some critical measurements, too. This 'cascading down' from the top-level processes is strongly recommended. Ownership of subprocesses means that they must have a defined future desired state, and it will be consistent with the *enterprise's* future desired state. The reward system should be changed accordingly, of course, so that the owners of subprocesses are rewarded for improving their subprocesses towards competitive excellence. Ultimately, this cascading down means that everyone in the enterprise knows the contribution they must make to increasing its Total Competitiveness.

Some questions for the owners of processes

More questions! Nevertheless, every manager should know the answers to these questions, today. The extent to which they are not known is a measure of lack of control. Answering them will identify some valuable opportunities for measuring processes.

1 How many iterations are needed to produce the process output — the trial balance, the invoice, the advertising copy, the income tax assessment, the piece of software?

(This question relates directly to costs and cycle times. The process owner really *must* find the answer to this question, then start to manage it downwards, if it is excessive. But what is excessive? See the next question.)

2 How does the answer to the above question compare with competitors? How does it compare with the best-of breed?

3 What are the biggest cost items in the process:

- within the enterprise (cross–charging)
- external to it (real money)?

What is the most rapidly growing cost item in the process?

4 What is the cost of quality (COQ) in the process?

(COQ = Prevention + Appraisal + Fixing cost.

Fixing costs are generally much higher than prevention costs or appraisal costs. And they are the most public. Fixing cost means the cost of fixing *after* the output has left the process, either to an internal customer (the trial balance, say) or to an external customer who receives a product that has defects, or an inaccurate, incomprehensible invoice.)

5 How many defects are reported each month, say, by:

- external customers
- internal customers
- internal suppliers
- external suppliers?

What are the defect trends? Increasing? Decreasing? In either case, what caused the increase or decrease?

6 How often do you review/negotiate the needs of your internal and external customers:

- every three months
- every six months
- yearly
- never
- only when the shouting starts?

You will probably be able to add your own questions to this incomplete list. The idea is not to create an immense measurement bureaucracy but to select just those key measurements that will be necessary and sufficient to enable the process owner to manage it to competitive excellence.

Measure what is important to *customers*.
Measure what is important to the *process*.
Measure what it is necessary to know to *improve* the process.

Statistical quality control

This is not the place for a detailed dissertation on statistical quality control. Neither is statistical quality control all about Japanese manufacturers relentlessly pursing 'zero defect' quality standards. Nevertheless, the statistical quality control ideas of W. Edwards Deming, who first visited Japan in 1947, have been credited with a large part of Japan's post-war economic miracle. It can be a useful tool for the owner of a business process.

Some of the process measurements will not be amenable to statistical quality control techniques. A measurement that is taken only once per month, for instance, is not appropriate, unless you are in the business of growing olive trees, say. But, other measurements — such as the time taken to respond to a customer's query or complaint, delivery performance, and so on — will need to be taken sufficiently frequently to merit using a statistical quality control approach.

It is not necessary to get into a lot of complicated arithmetic to use statistical quality control. You need only feed the data into a personal computer, for example, and it will produce a graphical display of the results.

The merit of statistical quality control is its honesty. With sufficient data (20 to 30 readings are enough to get started), it tells you what the process or activity is capable of doing *the way it is today*.

This is presented as an average level of performance, within a normal range of variations. And it will stay like this until the process owner imposes a *change* on the process. Statistical quality control knows nothing about targets. The process owner may set one target after another. The owner may shout and threaten. It makes no difference. Unless the *process* is somehow changed, the same results will appear. It simply reports the way things are. However, it can help the process owner make things better.

Any performance that is outside the boundaries of its normal range of variations is highlighted, and you only need those 20 to 30 initial readings to know what is 'normal'. Such deviations are statistically significant. Something unique, out of the ordinary, has happened for it to be this bad (or this good).

The process owner must find out what caused the unusually bad performance and remove the cause, so that it cannot happen again. Equally, the cause of the oustandingly *good* performance must also be determined — perhaps it can be permanently built into the process. This way, the average performance of the process improves and the boundaries of variability narrow. It really is as simple as this.

The process owner may then make a radical change to the process, in the interests of improvement. Then the owner has to wait for 20 to 30 new readings before statistical quality control can display the *new* average performance and the *new* boundaries of variability. As times passes, it will again highlight those statistically significant good and bad events for the owner to investigate. And so on, until the next dramatic change is imposed.

The Japanese call this process '*Kaizen*' — a sequence of radical improvements with periods of constant, incremental improvement in between. It works. It is worth considering, where it is appropriate.

> **The Cypress Semiconductor Corporation has instituted measurement systems *and* the means to prevent bad-quality products leaving the plant. Associated with their measurements, they have developed what they call 'killer software'. This automatically shuts down a manufacturing operation when it detects a violation of its usual high standards of performance. This has inspired dramatic improvements. People notice when part of the manufacturing plant stops.**
>
> **The killer software concept is being transferred to administrative processes involving order entry, accounts receivable, and so on.**

20

The endless journey towards Total Competitiveness

All of this focus on activities to improve the enterprise so it becomes more competitive will never stop. The changes in the business and political environment will guarantee that part of Doppler's conclusions will be invalidated a year from now. So, the seven key questions should be revisited once every year or so, even in the most tranquil times.

But, once the improvements start to be implemented it becomes much quicker and easier to change. I am assuming that Doppler stays in more or less the same industry. Even so, if it moves from retailing consumer electronics to manufacturing cement (unlikely), it would have some excellent processes in place that are truly cross-industry, such as 'Monitor the market-place', 'Monitor product quality', 'Review technology opportunities', 'Monitor personnel motivation'. The detail within each process might be different for the cement manufacturing business, but the essential elements — the skills and the systems to do the work of monitoring the quality of products excellently, for example — would be in place.

What follows is a somewhat idealized suggestion for what to do next. This said, it is only idealized to the extent that it assumes there are no major changes when Doppler revisits the seven key questions. Even so, the principles can still be applied after the possibly major real-world change has been addressed.

222

Let us take a final look at the definition of Total Competitiveness.

Total Competitiveness is the result of multiplying:

1 relative product price performance and

2 relative customer satisfaction with all customer-visible business processes.

'Relative' here means relative to the competition.

(Total Competitiveness will be used in the discussion that follows, but the same principles apply to Total Effectiveness.)

The *distinction* between invisible and customer-visible processes is important, but neither group is more important than the other. Here is Doppler's original list of 11 critical business processes, together with an indication of visibility:

- Define market strategies   Invisible
- Procure products   Invisible
- Order products for warehouses   Invisible
- Order products for stores   Invisible
- Merchandize products   Customer-visible
- Monitor the competition   Invisible
- Monitor product quality   Customer-visible
  (Doppler explicitly
  wants the customer to
  participate in this
  process)
- Monitor customer complaints   Customer-visible
- Review technology opportunities   Invisible
- Identify/cultivate key opinion
  formers   Invisible
- Monitor personnel motivation   Invisible

Three of these processes are customer-visible; eight are invisible. It just turned out this way. But it reveals something about the management team's collective views and concerns at the time of the study. This 3:8 ratio is very inward-looking — *and this was correct for Doppler Electronics at that time.* Clearly, there needed to be a focus on the internals of the business, to reduce costs, improve responsiveness, and so on. It was a natural consequence of this particular team answering these seven key questions at that particular time.

Another management team, working for one of Doppler's competitors, might produce a list with eight customer-visible processes and only three invisible ones. This would indicate a team that is probably running an efficient and tight ship, but people have stopped coming on board. Focusing on *Total* Competitiveness reveals the need to do something about these customer-visible processes. Again the 8 : 3 ratio is *correct at the time* for the second management team.

Figure 20.1 shows a way of representing Doppler's ratio and that of its competitor. We could call Doppler's profile 'business operations orientated' and the competitor's profile 'market orientated'. The Doppler team would object strenuously if anyone tried to tell it that it was *not* market orientated, by the way. Every member of the management team has an almost fanatical concern about serving customers. This, though, is not the issue. What it reveals is that the major opportunities for improving Total Competitiveness, at the time of their study, were within the business, invisible to customers, despite the team's devotion to its customers.

No doubt the competitor's team would equally strenuously deny that it was operations orientated. It just turns out that *their* major competitiveness opportunities will be customer-visible.

Companies can oscillate between being operations orientated and market orientated. And, quite often, the oscillations are violent. The market orientated company gains market share, has satisfied customers, good revenues. Then someone says, 'We are not making any profit!' Budget cuts follow, across the board. Big cost-saving programmes are put in place. The reward system changes to reflect the new approach. It works. But, market shares decrease. Revenues start to fall. Then someone says, 'We are losing customers!' Everyone then

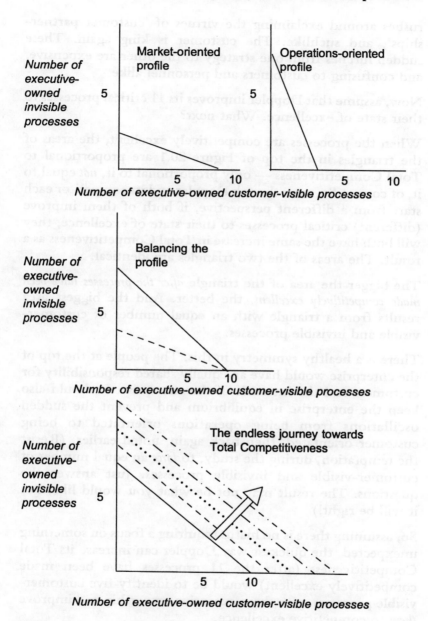

Figure 20.1 Representations of the two different profiles and what needs to be done to move enterprises towards Total Competitiveness

rushes around exclaiming the virtues of 'customer partnerships', and suchlike. The customer is king again. These sudden lurches from one strategy to the other are expensive, and confusing to customers and personnel alike.

Now, assume that Doppler improves its 11 critical processes to their state of excellence. What next?

When the processes are competitively excellent, the areas of the triangles in the top of Figure 20.1 are proportional to Total Competitiveness — only proportional to it, *not* equal to it, of course. So, even though Doppler and its competitor each start from a different perspective, if both of them improve (different) critical processes to their state of excellence, they will both have the same increase in Total Competitiveness as a result. The areas of the two triangles are identical.

The bigger the area of the triangle *after the processes have been made competitively excellent*, the better. And the biggest area results from a triangle with an equal number of customer-visible and invisible processes.

There is a healthy symmetry in this. The people at the top of the enterprise would have an equally shared responsibility for customers and the internals of the enterprise. It should also keep the enterprise in equilibrium and prevent the sudden oscillations from being operations orientated to being customer orientated, then back again, noted earlier. (Resist the temptation, during the study, to *force* an equal number of customer-visible and invisible processes. Just answer the questions. The result may not be what you would like, but it will be right!)

So, assuming there is no hiatus requiring a focus on something unexpected, the quickest way Doppler can increase its Total Competitiveness (after the 11 processes have been made competitively excellent) would be to identify five customer-visible processes, give them executive ownership and improve *them* to competitive excellence.

Does this mean that the top-management team now has active

ownership of 16 business processes? Not necessarily. The additional 5 processes are added *only* after the original 11 have been made excellent, and these should then be stable. *Then,* management of some of the stable, excellent processes may be delegated down one level.

When the additional five customer-visible processes have been improved to excellence, Doppler's triangle now looks like that in the centre of Figure 20.1. Total Competitiveness has increased.

What next?

Identify two more invisible processes, say, and two more customer-visible processes, delegate management of four existing excellent processes, and improve the new ones to competitive excellence. And so on (see the illustration at the bottom of Figure 20.1)

This keeps the balance between what is important to customers and what is important to the internals of the enterprise, while continually improving its Total Competitiveness/Effectiveness. It will be led from the top. And there will always be a new, unexploited opportunity.

The journey will never end.

Bon voyage!

Appendix: a cross-referenced list of business processes

This is a selection of business processes, cross-referenced to the enterprises that have had some success in making them more competitive. They are all drawn from available published sources.

The purpose of this list is to help you in designing your own projects for improving Total Competitiveness/Effectiveness, whether or not they can be classed as re-engineering projects. Some examples may be copied directly into your own enterprise. Better yet, use them to trigger your own imagination, to create something original that will truly differentiate your enterprise from your competitors.

By every process is the relevant page number in the Appendix where you will find a description of the enterprise's approach to this process. Where a reference has already been described in the body of the book, it is not repeated here. Instead, the page number for where it appears is given so you can recap.

Business process	Page	Enterprise
Allocate production	241	The Merrill Corporation
Answer customer queries	235	American President Companies
	188	Bausch and Lomb
	89	General Electric
	236	United Services Automobile Association
Bill customers	242	British Rail
	232	DuPont

Enterprise: Airtours
Process: Price products

Airtours is the UK's second-biggest travel company.

A team of ten people adjusts prices all day to maximize the profitability of its share of the UK's £4.5 billion air holiday market. Price adjustments have to be made to reflect the time of year, the demand, the UK weather, the availability of aircraft seats (an empty seat means a loss) and what competitors are charging. This means that Airtours does not necessarily follow a competitor down in price.

Airtours has access to competitors' prices through its ownership of the Going Places chain of travel agents, and this also gives them information about how well its competitors' products are selling. Airtours' two major competitors change prices every night; Airtours does it several times a day.

Enterprise: DuPont
Processes: Bill customers
Distribute products
Monitor quality
Pay suppliers
Process customer orders
Procure parts and raw materials

Through EDI (Electronic Data Interchange) DuPont is sending and receiving purchase orders, purchase order acknowledgements, material releases, advance shipping notices, invoices, remittance and payment advice, bills of lading, freight invoices, and quality control data.

In addition, DuPont offers customers a variety of specialized information services. These include electronic mail, quality data, computer-aided design and engineering, status of orders, materials specifications, and business management tools.

DuPont receives about 2000 electronic freight invoices each business day, from about 40 rail and motor carriers. This has reduced the front-end freight payment processing cost by 50 per cent and enables DuPont to comply with payment terms for all undisputed freight invoices.

(*Note*: The EDI system was funded from the corporate budget because strategic management viewed it as a strategic investment opportunity.)

Enterprises: Nippon Seiko
Mazak Machinery
Fujitsu Fanuc

Processes: Manufacture products
Process customer orders
Schedule production

NSK (Nippon Seiko), which manufactures bearings, has virtually removed its workforce by means of the extensive use of computer-integrated manufacturing that is linked directly to the market-place. Its plant in Fukishama is one of the most automated in the world. Computer-controlled inventory systems link all of its nine Japanese factories. (In January 1990, it acquired UPI, the UK's biggest bearing manufacturer. This doubled its small market share in Europe and provided it with six more manufacturing sites.)

Using a similar approach, Mazak Machinery has taken almost all of the labour content out of key components in its products.

Fujitsu Fanuc has so streamlined itself that it has publicly announced that it can break even with as little as 20 per cent capacity utilization and can compete successfully with a currency as strong as 70 yen to the American dollar.

Enterprises: Hercules
Ford
Westinghouse

Process: Convey internal communications

Hercules is a chemical company with headquarters in Wilmington, Delaware, USA. Its sales are over $3 billion. It sells over 1000 products and operates 40 US plants and 24 sales offices. Of its 26 000 employees in 80 locations worldwide, only 10 per cent live in the Wilmington area.

Hercules holds frequent video meetings in 25 video conferencing rooms — 5 at its headquarters building and 20 in other domestic and international offices. It found that video conferencing '... not only saves time and travel, it forces us to make the meetings more organized. And we get a chance to exchange information that otherwise would wait. Meetings are held more frequently.'

Hercules has been able to cut out 6 or 7 entire layers of management. Routing text around offices worldwide has reduced secretarial costs by 40 per cent, a saving of $3 million a year.

A study by Ford of Europe found that participants in a one-hour video meeting accomplished what usually took four hours. It also reported highly effective 15-minute meetings that it would have been impractical to hold any other way.

Westinghouse's electronic mail efforts began in 1980. Today, there are 6000 PCs connecting 10 000 managers and employees and 1000 customers in 38 countries.

Electronic mail costs 90 per cent less than overseas calls and mail, and 75 per cent less than telex. Time zone differences can be used effectively this way so that one zone, say Japan, is working on solutions to questions from the USA so responses can be delivered to the USA in time for its next working day.

These tools contributed up to one third of the 6 per cent annual increases in Westinghouse's productivity since the early 1980s. White–collar workers have increased in numbers to form 73 per cent of the total number of workers from 43 per cent 25 years ago.

Enterprises: British Airways
                  Waitrose
Process: Educate/train employees

British Airways has links with the University of Lancaster that go back to 1988. Since then, over 200 managers have participated in its corporate education programme. British Airways claims that it has identified clear benefits over the years, including an improvement in the quality of management, greater functional mobility among employees, the development of a learning culture, and the growth of effective networks among participants.

Over 1000 electronic point of sale trainees at Waitrose can now learn more in less time with a multimedia training package. The food shops of the UK's John Lewis Partnership have added this package to its integrated training programme. The interactive programme designed by MediaSys combines graphics, photographic material, voiceover and music with company procedures. Roger Collins, MediaSys's general manager claims there is a 25 per cent rise in information retained and training time can be cut by 35 per cent.

Enterprise: American President Companies (APC)
Processes: Answer customer queries
Distribute products
Monitor inventory movements
Track vehicle movements

A network of satellites and land-based communication links enables APC to track cargo movements throughout Asia and North America. A customer can call an APC computer on a toll-free number. A digitized voice helps the caller to enter the query and then speaks the location of the customer's shipment within 10 seconds.

The justification for this system was not the reduction of costs. APC wanted to make better decisions about how to route its ships, trains and trucks: 'Our Bombay office moved from the seventeenth to the twentieth century!' Offering the free voice response system was a relatively low-cost additional innovation that increased customer service — and differentiation from its competitors.

APC performs an essential part of the parts distribution process for the Ford Motor Company, between its plants in Woodhaven, Michigan, and Hermosillo, in Mexico.

APC coordinates all the information, transportation, and inventory handling necessary to collect parts and components from suppliers and sequence them into containers for delivery on a Just-In-Time basis to Hermosillo. The process includes coordination over four railway companies and with Mexican customs officials for delay-free clearance. Ford and APC collaborate to return containers to the US carrying components produced in the Maquiladora region of Mexico.

APC also uses its information technology platform to link clothing manufacturers in the Far East with the interior of North America. The service offers container delivery of goods on hangers that are sequenced in size and colour to each particular retailer's specifications, before being loaded in Asia.

Enterprise: United Services Automobile Association (USAA)
Processes: Answer customer queries
                Maintain customer records

USAA manages the equivalent of 300 million pages of image data for more than 1000 terminals and 2000 users.

One year of mail and computer output from this insurance company requires about 20 000 square feet (1860 square metres) of office space. Six more years of mail are stored in a warehouse.

Charles Plessums, Manager of image systems at USAA, calculated that he could store 7 years of documents on 25 square feet (2.3 square metres) of optical disk.

A video showing the system claims the following advantages:

- *Service*: queries are handled in minutes rather than days
- *Productivity*: much easier access to files, fewer telephone call-backs, many people can access the same document at the same time, and easier to supervise.
- *Money*: $4 million from the expected savings in space and personnel and optimization of workflow/prioritization of work.

USAA's Chief Executive, Robert F. Mcdermott, said, 'I

236

wanted to get rid of paper. All our files were lying in folders and access to any particular piece of paper was only possible after up to a month of searching. So, I started burning the files to demonstrate my commitment and to show there would be no turning back.'

An estimated 160 employees once involved in file-handling were retrained for other more dignified and profitable positions.

McDermott credited the use of image processing, expert systems, and networks with reducing the cost of processing policies. USAA's underwriting expense ratio (the cost of underwriting policies divided by the values of the premiums written) is 9 per cent. The nearest competitor's ratio in the same industry is 13 per cent.

Enterprise: Celltech
Process: Manufacture pharmaceutical products

In a new pharmaceutical factory, 4 robots, sealed in stainless steel cells, are performing a delicate manoeuvre that might otherwise have needed as many as 50 highly trained staff.

Celltech has adopted a novel solution to the problem of scaling up the manufacture of a new drug. The process involves the mass culture of mammalian cells to make a therapeutic hormone.

To achieve the planned output, Celltech was faced with the choice of recruiting 40 to 50 graduates for a single stage of the process or mimicking their manipulations mechanically. As the procedure had been approved by the drug regulatory authorities, it could not be changed without requiring revalidation. This would have incurred a two-year delay.

Celltech called in the Technology Partnership, Cambridge (UK), consulting engineers. The consultants saw it initially as a 'one-off' assignment because it believed that the roller-bottle concept of manufacture (used in the Celltech process) was obsolescent. It has since learned that roller bottles continue to be used for vaccine manufacture, a highly labour-intensive activity.

Each robot system processes between 150 and 200 bottles an hour. They run seven days a week under the eye of a single supervisor, with just two operators to load and unload them.

Enterprise: Milliken
Processes: Process customer orders
Procure parts/raw materials
Manufacture products
Schedule production

Milliken is a large US textile manufacturer. It has extended beyond its own organizational boundaries to include customers and suppliers in one, integrated delivery system.

Milliken and its customers can share order input and scheduling information, coordinate production to minimize imbalances, and eliminate duplicate inspections and buffer inventories.

Costs have fallen. Inventory turns have typically doubled. Stock shortages and markdowns occur less often. The time it takes the Milliken customer to fill an order has been cut in half.

Enterprise: British Petroleum
Process: Invest liquid funds

British Petroleum manages its own financial transactions and, therefore, saves on commission. Even as long ago as 1986, British Petroleum Finance International managed the company's $4 billion of liquid resources and contributed over $40 million to its annual income. It used telecommunications so that it could become a bank.

Enterprise: Union Bank of Switzerland
Processes: Maintain customer records
Monitor security of sensitive material

Optical disk technology is used to store and retrieve customer

238

signatures — 250 000 of them — for the Zurich region, initially.

When a payment order is received, the user keys in the account number and calls up the relevant signature card, previously scanned and stored on optical disk for display. At the same time, brief details of the account can be displayed.

Signature verification is much faster this way than it was with the old system. In addition, more than one request can be handled simultaneously and the turnaround of customer requests is now much faster. An additional benefit is better control of accounts and the effective prevention of signature cards being lost, damaged or wrongly filed.

Enterprise: First Boston Corporation
Process: Process loan applications

SHELTERNET is an electronic information exchange system offered by First Boston Corporation. It allows real estate brokers to determine quickly and easily what mortgage packages are available and whether or not the buyer will qualify for financing. This improves the position of both the brokers and the homebuyers in shopping for mortgages. The parties can make preliminary commitments within 30 minutes.

Enterprise: Metroteller Systems Inc.
Processes: Process loan applications
               Process customer banking instructions

Metroteller was formed in 1975. It was the first in the USA to link up the ATM networks operated by the individual banks.

Customers may now apply and get approval for car loans within minutes of signing a purchase agreement. This also helps dealers to keep customers who might otherwise withdraw from a sale before the loan is approved. It also gives customers better loan rates by allowing dealers to submit on–line applications to several banks.

Car dealers can use the system to authorize cheques, debit

customers' current or savings accounts, and authorize credit card payments for customers making downpayments or paying for servicing or repairs. The system has been installed in 4000 dealerships and 1000 banks.

Enterprise: A bank in Philadelphia, USA
Processes: Process loan applications
Market products/services

A bank in Philadelphia supports a 24-hour-a-day car loan service using information technology. Competitors were forced to respond or lose market share. Those who responded before their support systems were ready found that their loan losses rose.

The original innovator was determined to keep the initiative. Eventually, customers were able to take their choice of car out for a test drive and, if the car was fitted with a mobile telephone, have their loan approved before returning to the showroom.

The bank extended the system — people are predictable. The system was able to anticipate when good customers would need a change of car. It sent them unsolicited cheques with an invitation to deposit the cash if they needed the loan.

Enterprise: Banque Populaire du Midi
Process: Process customer banking transactions

Banque Populaire du Midi (BPM) has set itself the ambitious objective of achieving the same coverage with its videotex banking services as the PTT, France Télécom.

Clients can do much more than simply look at their bank statement at any time. They may also look at each individual account, be given a historic view of their account(s) over several months, allocate funds from one account to another, perform budget analysis, and so forth.

Videotex allows the Bank to offer these services without placing any obligation on the client to make any commitment to the Bank.

After 3 years' experience, 15 per cent of clients are using the service. Benefits include:

- increased customer loyalty — BPM claims that videotex customer loyalty is ten times that of other clients
- the ability to penetrate companies that are not normally customers of BPM
- 5 per cent of BPM's staff can be released to do other market-orientated work
- the image of BPM has been enhanced, not only with customers, but also within the Bank.

Enterprise: Citicorp
Processes: Market products/services
Process customer banking transactions

Chemical Bank was the first to install ATMs in New York, in 1969. The goal was simply to automate the teller's job — the focus was on reducing costs. It did not work, so Chemical withdrew.

Citicorp saw ATMs as a marketing tool. It did a lot of research on customer responses and created much friendlier machines. By covering the city with them in the late 1970s, it more than doubled its current and deposit accounts and increased its market share from 5 to 13 per cent.

Enterprise: The Merrill Corporation
(This company has no connection with Merrill Lynch)
Processes: Procure services
Offer services for sale
Allocate production

Merrill is a printing company in the US that specializes in financial printing, such as mergers, financial prospectus documents, and so on. Its 1988 revenue was $55 million, with $2 million profit. It was originally a local company, operating in the twin towns of St Paul and Minneapolis.

When its niche market came under attack from larger

national companies, it fought back and won, using telecommunications and information technology.

It can now tie its typesetting operations in St Paul to offices and printing plants in 11 cities in the USA. Merrill can compete for contracts to supply documents virtually anywhere in the country. It uses its telecommunications network to connect typesetters and proofreaders (Merrill's suppliers) appropriate to the demand.

Merrill works with at least three printers in each market and is usually one of the printer's best customers. It also tends to use the normally least utilized third shift. Because Merrill is such a good customer, printers will stop other jobs and put Merrill's material on the presses.

The network has been in place since 1982; sales multiplied seven times between 1983 and 1988.

Customers work at Merrill's remote conference facilities through up to 13 drafts, on-line, before the final proof is sent electronically to the Securities and Exchange Commission and to the chosen printer.

'In effect, we are a $55 million a year company that has more than $400 million worth of printing capacity', says John Castro, Merrill's President, and one of the three people who developed the system.

Enterprise: British Rail
Processes: Track vehicle movements
Bill customers

British Rail has bought industrial PCs for an automatic vehicle identification project (AVI).

At offices beside the track, each computer is connected to a monitoring system so trains can be automatically identified as they pass by. This reduces the costs of tracking vehicles, currently done manually. It also improves the accuracy of billing freight customers, as the systems are connected to automatic weighbridges.

(*Note*: Some European railways operate with 20 to 30 per cent more trucks than they need to because they do not know where they all are.)

Enterprise: Image Directe
Process: Offer products for sale

Image Directe has been formed by the illustrator Tribun and the photographic agency Kipa. Using the 64 Kbit ISDN service, it offers a digitized image service to subscribers, who are given special terminals. Journalists, advertisers, television companies, and so on can call up images from a central database (which will contain about a million images), manipulate them, call up complete documentation on each, and use the images directly for publishing and other purposes.

Enterprise: Service SA
Processes: Maintain installed products
Monitor product quality

Service SA is a French subsidiary of Philips Group. It supplies after-sales service for consumer goods sold in France.

It is an early user of the ISDN service, which offers much higher data transmission speeds than conventional switched data lines.

It supplies pictures that support, interactively, the textual element of a service expert system, which has been designed specifically for helping dealers (who are Service SA's customers) to repair products. The direct cost saving is 10 per cent. Additionally, the system enables statistical data on repairs to be fed back to Quality Control, for example, and to production units. This may be ten minutes after diagnosing the fault, compared with two months the old way.

Enterprise: Royal Institute of British Architects
Processes: Design new products
Offer products for sale

Architects using computer-aided design (CAD) systems no longer need to draw toilet bowls or remember the dimensions of bricks. Their CAD workstations invariably arrive with a library of such drawings supplied by the Royal Institute of British Architects (RIBA).

About 40 companies making building products — including Twyfords, Marley, Ideal Standard, and so on — pay RIBA Services Limited up to £20 000 to be included in its RibaCad database, and so get their merchandise displayed in front of buyers.

When architects were surveyed by the RIBA, 60 per cent confirmed that their product choices were influenced if they were given a drawing. Alan Ray-Jones, RIBA Services' Technical Director, says that there is an overwhelming demand for this facility.

Enterprise: Hewlett-Packard
Process: Market products

Hewlett-Packard has developed a 'closed loop' sales and marketing system for internal use. It is an integrated web of a complicated database, customer information centre (CIC), communications and sales force applications.

The result of this programme in the US, is that selling time has increased by 27 per cent, enquiry volumes have risen by 72 per cent (with only 10 per cent of leads being discarded), and direct marketing costs have been cut by 10 per cent. The company now gets feedback on 90 per cent of sales, something that was almost non-existent before.

Hewlett-Packard's closed loop creates a virtuous circle. Direct Marketing, for example, initiates an enquiry. This is qualified as a lead and fed to the sales channels. The subsequent win or loss is reported to the customer database, which generates management information that helps to improve the next marketing effort: 'The system just gets smarter and smarter'.

Enterprise: Seven-Eleven
Processes: Monitor consumer buying patterns
Distribute products

Procure products
Offer products for sale

Seven-Eleven is Japan's largest food retailer. There are about 3900 Seven-Eleven convenience stores. Most of them are owned by franchise holders. 1988 sales were $4 billion, and profitability and return on equity are the highest among Japanese retailers.

With an average of only 100 square metres of shelf space and over 3500 products to move at any one time, store owners need to know what to sell and when. The shelves are filled with a mix of goods according to the time of day.

Seven-Eleven uses a sophisticated computer network to collect sales statistics and order goods directly from distributors.

Seven-Eleven the company is little more than its network. The parent, a subsidiary of Japanese retailer Ito-Yokado, owns only about 5 per cent of the stores, and even this small proportion is decreasing.

Each store is equipped with a clever cash register. These are also owned by Seven-Eleven so it can control technical standards across the network. When something is bought, the machine notes its brand name, the manufacturer, the price, and the sex and age of the buyer. Each machine is fitted with a special monitor that displays information in the form of charts to the shopkeepers. Sales of a certain product can be plotted against the time of day, day of the week, and so on. This way, patterns can easily be identified and new products tested.

Shopkeepers can send orders from the cash register (it is also a computer terminal), directly to suppliers. The only paper they see is a delivery note. They can also see whether or not a supplier has a given item in stock. With three deliveries a day, an order can be at the store within eight hours of it being placed.

Seven-Eleven can also aggregate the statistics from many

stores. It sells statistics to manufacturers about the sales of their *own* products, but it will not reveal anything about the sales of a *rival* manufacturer's products. The statistics also enable Seven-Eleven to advise their franchise holders on what to sell and when, thereby binding them into the organization.

Seven-Eleven owns only the network design and the sales terminals. The telephone lines are of normal capacity. Even the mainframe computer is rented.

Enterprise: Frito-Lay
Processes: Monitor product sales performance
                Monitor inventories
                Market products

Frito-Lay is a division of PepsiCo Inc. The source of this information is its President and Chief Executive. Its products are snack foods.

Until recently, Frito-Lay had a centralized decision-making structure. Product information moved slowly up through the organization — too slowly to be really effective. It could not respond quickly to changes in its rapidly changing markets or manage its inventory effectively.

A dramatic change in this situation resulted from its Decision Support System (DSS) introduced in 1989. DSS provides detailed sales and inventory information to 200 managers. The data is entered by 10 000 salespeople via hand-held computers.

For the sales force, it saves an estimated 30 000 hours a week in total, plus there are considerable savings in clerical costs and the costs of paper forms and postage.

But, most important, 'DSS gives gives us the information we need, not what someone wants to give after it has been massaged and sanitized. And we get it when we want it, which is usually immediately.' Top management can see within a few days which products are selling well, and which are not, enabling it to devise a strategy immediately: 'I never thought a computer would be responsible for a total reorganization of

Frito–Lay, but it has been. DSS allows middle managers to have a complete picture of what is happening in their regions. Now about 60 per cent of the decisions formerly made by top management are made by regional managers.'

Enterprise: Nippon Telephone and Telegraph/Toto
Process: Monitor body functions

'Smart' toilets with perfumed sprays, warm air dryers, heated seats, music, and so on have been available in Japan for some time. More than 4 million have been sold. A strategic alliance between Nippon Telephone And Telegraph and Toto, a sanitary ware manufacturer, has resulted in intelligent toilets, connected on–line to a central computer.

Sensors measure weight, temperature, pulse and so on, and perform urine analysis for sugar level, protein, urobilinogen, occult blood in urine, and so on. A monitor displays the results. The toilet stores 130 days' worth of readings, prints them out, transfers them to a PC or transmits them to a medical service for further analysis. Emergency services can be called out automatically and a hospital placed in readiness.

Work is proceeding to identify users by their 'seatprint'.

Each toilet costs about $7000. They are being introduced into the United States.

Enterprise: Progressive Insurance
Process: Process insurance claims

Progressive Insurance has been experimenting with an 'office van'. The van includes a PC with modem, printer, fax and two cellular phones, together with soft chairs and refreshments. The idea is to arrive at the scene of an accident within 15 minutes and settle the claim within a maximum of 90 minutes, including payment.

When physical injury is not involved, the insured is invited into the van and offered a soft drink while the report is filed and verified. The claims adjuster photographs the damage and

247

transmits it by a cellular fax machine to a central claims estimation service.

A cheque is issued on the spot.

This cuts down on office expenses, towing charges, and storage, and eliminates additional expenses incurred by involving lawyers. The adjuster then offers to arrange to tow the vehicle to a garage that will guarantee to repair the damage for the amount of the cheque and guarantee the quality of the work. The adjuster also offers the customer a lift to their destination and arranges for a vehicle to be loaned, if needed. Customer satisfaction is increased. (Progressive has been growing at 20 per cent per year since 1988, and making good profits, too.)

Results have been encouraging, so far. Progressive would like their vans to become as familiar a sight as those from Federal Express, for example.

Enterprises: Securicor/George Wimpy
Volback
Processes: Monitor security/infractions
Track vehicle movements

A gang of thieves who stole a truck full of cigarettes worth £300 000 were somewhat surprised when the police intercepted them almost immediately. A vehicle tracking system, developed jointly by Securicor and George Wimpy called Datatrak, had been monitoring their progress across London. A transmitter attached to the vehicle's chassis gave information regarding its location to a remote computerized tracking system.

A similar facility is available in France, where more than 12 000 cars have been equipped with such a system. It is marketed under the name Volback and lower insurance premiums can be negotiated by owners of vehicles so equipped. A similar system in the UK has insurance companies offering between 7 and 15 per cent discounts on premiums. In France in 1993, the recovery rate for stolen cars equipped with this technology was about 85 per cent.

Index